For Alan, David and Gillian

DAN DONNELLY

1788–1820

Pugilist, Publican, Playboy

Patrick Myler

THE LILLIPUT PRESS
DUBLIN

First edition published in hardback as
Regency Rogue: Dan Donnelly, his life and legends,
by The O'Brien Press, Dublin, in 1976,
and in paperback in 1978

Revised edition published 2010 by
THE LILLIPUT PRESS
62–63 Sitric Road, Arbour Hill
Dublin 7, Ireland
www.lilliputpress.ie

ISBN 978 1 84351 158 8

1 3 5 7 9 10 8 6 4 2

A CIP record for this title is available
from The British Library.

Set in 12 pt on 17 pt Baskerville by Marsha Swan
Printed in Ireland by ColourBooks of Dublin

Contents

Preface   ix
Acknowledgments   xiii

1. The Sack-'em-Ups Strike   3
2. The People's Champion   16
3. Beating a Bully   25
4. King of the Curragh   38
5. Cooper's Challenge   50
6. Publican and Playboy   73
7. Facing the Sceptical English   81
8. Training – It's a Bore!   92
9. The Battle with Tom Oliver   98
10. Paying the Penalty   115
11. The Prince Regent and 'Sir Daniel'   123
12. Donnybrook Fair   136
13. The Fatal Knockout   147
14. But Not Forgotten   157

Afterword   171
    Donnelly's Hollow Monument   171
    Dan's Pipe and Jug Sold at Auction   178
    Donnelly Recalled on Stage   181
    Encounter with a 'Ghost'   182
    A Favourite of Jack B. Yeats   183

Plaque Erected at Last Residence   183

Elected to Hall of Fame   185

Dan's Arm on Tour   185

Bibliography   189

Index   193

Preface

It is over forty years since I first shook Dan Donnelly by the hand – well, I held his mummified right arm, which is the next best thing! I can remember my mixed feelings on being 'introduced' to the Irish prizefighting hero by the late Jim Byrne Junior, who proudly displayed his unique keepsake in a glass case at his pub, The Hideout, in Kilcullen, County Kildare. My initial queasiness gave way to elation at the realization that I was reaching into history via the once-powerful right arm that had served to inspire an Irish nation hungering for self-government as he conquered his English foes two centuries ago.

Had I been around then, I would have enthusiastically joined the crowds as they journeyed from far and near, using every horse-drawn conveyance available, or happily made the journey on foot, to witness his barefist battles on the Curragh of Kildare. After cheering him to victory, I would have taken my turn to follow the champion as he strode up the slope of Donnelly's Hollow and helped carve out the imprints that remain intact to this day, alongside the monument commemorating his historic successes.

While it cannot legitimately be claimed that Donnelly rates among the all-time greats of boxing, no man who ever stepped into a roped square to test his strength and courage against an opponent is as well feted in story, in legend, and in song. By his exploits in the ring, he symbolized Ireland's fight from freedom from British domination every time he bloodied an English nose.

There are those who insist he owes his fame more to myth than fact. Certainly some of the stories told about him – the knighthood granted by the Prince Regent, the arms so long that he could fasten his knee-breeches without stooping, his invincibility in the ring – are apocryphal, but there is no denying the impact he made on the sporting and social scene in the early years of the nineteenth century.

Much of what has been written about Donnelly portrays him as the archetypal Irishman, devil-may-care, good humoured, with a roving eye and an over-fondness for alcohol. The conclusions may not be too far from the truth, but when I first undertook to write his biography in 1976, I purposely set out to separate fact and fiction, as best as I could, and ascertain why the idol of the poor had also won widespread admiration from the nobility. His brave exploits and outgoing personality clearly had a way of breaking down class barriers.

In attempting an honest appraisal of Donnelly's life, I have managed to expose many of the legends adhering to his name. Where there is no proof for or against a story, I have given the accounts as I found them. That he stood out as a 'celebrity' in the colourful, often outlandish, Regency period says much for the impact he made on the Irish and English scene.

Donnelly's arm, cut off after his grave was raided, has been preserved for almost 200 years. Courtesy Josephine Byrne.

Acknowledgments

At the time of my original research into Donnelly's life, I tried – and failed – to find any living descendants. In the intervening years, several members of the wider Donnelly family, all from outside Ireland, contacted me seeking information, or offering to share their own findings with me. I am grateful for their continuing interest and hope I have helped to fill in some of the gaps in their famous ancestor's story.

Kathleen Romig Krepps, of Washington DC, is a direct descendant of Frances Donnelly, Dan's sister. Family research revealed that when Frances, aged seventeen, married John Collins, it was her little brother, Dan, who acted as the ring-bearer. Tragically, Frances died just after the birth of her sixth child. Her widowed husband went to work in England and sent most of his earnings home to support his family in Ardee, County Meath. Surviving letters refer to his visits home every Christmas, when Uncle Dan from Dublin would entertain the children, show them how to box and play the game of fives. The house would be filled with laughter at their antics, the letters recall. Frances Donnelly Collins was the great-great-grandmother of Kathleen Romig Krepps, who named her son, born on 15 June 2008, Daniel Donnelly Krepps, in memory of her illustrious ancestor.

Dan Donnelly, a researcher with BBC Wales, is planning to make a radio documentary on his famous ancestor. His grandfather, who believed he was the pugilist's great-great-grandson, was a prominent amateur boxer in the 1930s and was Lancashire and Cheshire champion. He was known as Tom 'One-Round' Donnelly for his record of quick knockouts. Becky Harvey, from Yorkshire, claims to be a descendant of Donnelly's and she remembers her grandfather had unusually long arms!

I owe my appreciation to Josephine Byrne, current owner of Donnelly's arm, James J. Houlihan, curator of The Fighting Irishmen exhibition, Andrew Gallimore, who wrote and directed an excellent TV documentary on Donnelly for TG4, Dr Simon Chaplin, Director of Museums and Special Collections, Royal College of Surgeons, London, for describing the methods of preserving human specimens in the early nineteenth century, Tommy Kiernan, for 'introducing' me to Donnelly's arm, Tony Gee, Clay Moyle, Noel Garnham, Nick McBride, Michael Taub, and Ron Jackson. I also thank the Estate of Jack B. Yeats for permission to reproduce several of the artist's works, along with The O'Brien Press, my original publisher, and The Lilliput Press, my current publisher.

Dan Donnelly (1788–1820)

ONE

The Sack-'em-Ups Strike

A sense of shock and revulsion gripped the visiting group as they entered the Hospital Fields burial ground – popularly known as Bully's Acre – at Kilmainham, less than two miles west of Dublin city centre, on the bitterly cold morning of 21 February 1821. They found loose earth strewn around the grave, which lay wide open, confirming their worst fears. The Sack-'em-Ups had come calling.

It would cause a national outcry when the news got out. Body snatching might be such a common occurrence that another instance would largely go unnoticed, but this was no ordinary mortal whose last resting place had been desecrated. The corpse crudely dragged from the grave with ropes, dumped into a sack and loaded onto a horse-drawn cart for transportation to a predestined location, was that

This drawing of Dan Donnelly, 'The Greatest Fighter of Them All' (1934), by New Yorker Joseph Carney, bore the legend that Dan's arms were so long he could button his knee-breeches without stooping. Courtesy Josephine Byrne.

of Dan Donnelly, pugilistic champion of Ireland, and a national folk hero.

Word of the outrage spread like wildfire. The public, already in deep mourning after Donnelly's sudden death at the unfathomably early age of thirty-two, could scarcely believe anyone would be so evil as to deny their champion his sleep of peace. They remembered how he had raised the flagging spirits of the downtrodden Irish by his stirring victories over highly regarded English prizefighters, of how he had so impressed the Prince Regent, later to become King George IV, that he was supposedly awarded a knight-hood, and how, after his great triumph over George Cooper on the Curragh of Kildare, his footsteps had been carved out of the turf at the place known to the present day as Donnelly's Hollow.

Much of the blame for allowing the raid to take place was attributed to the slack attitude of those who had been appointed as grave minders. They might have gone there with the best intentions, but the bitterness of the weather and the close location of a warm, comfortable tavern had warped their judgment. Their dereliction of duty was con-demned by J. Burrows, of 73 Baggot Street, Dublin, in a letter to *Carrick's Morning Post* published on 23 February:

> Having attended the remains of the victorious Donnelly
> to his last home on Sunday, a curiosity of again beholding
> his grave induced me, on passing that way this evening,
> to turn into the ground accompanied by two friends.
> On coming to the Hero's grave, what was our surprise
> to behold the clay thrown up, the coffin lid broken and

the body gone. It immediately occurred to us that the Resurrectionists of York Street had paid him a visit. We passed through Kilmainham and were informed that during the last two nights a few admirers of his art had been there to protect him, but their naturally jovial disposition and the severity of the weather prompted them to take too frequent libations on the tomb of the departed champion and disabled them from perceiving or opposing those riflers of the House of Death.

Denials that Donnelly's grave had been violated failed to pacify the angry public. Minor disturbances broke out and the authorities were afraid the trouble might escalate. The police were ordered to spare no efforts in bringing the perpetrators to justice and recovering the body, but they proved inadequate to the task. Suspicion for the foul deed fell on many sides. Morgan O'Doherty, in a letter to *Blackwood's Magazine*, told of some Dublin students being targeted and beaten up by a gang. The writer, expressing the general sense of frustration at the lack of information, added: 'It is absolutely impossible to ascertain the facts about the whereabouts of Donnelly's body. You hear a thousand times a day that it has been taken to Edinburgh.'

In an attempt to cool public passions, a group of publican friends of the late champion penned a letter to *The Freeman's Journal* claiming that the story of the grave robbery was a hoax. They wrote:

An article appeared in *Carrick's Morning Post* with the signature of a respectable individual annexed stating that the body had been removed from its place of interment.

We, on Thursday the 24th, visited the grave and, having it opened, found the body safe and undisturbed. As a further security we have had a temporary arch erected over it.

The letter was signed by Patrick Cody (no address given), P. Bergin (Fleet Street), Joseph Bergin (Essex Street), R. Gregson (Moore Street), Peter Kelly (Wood Quay), Garrett Graham (Cook Street), Byrne (Cole's Lane Market), and Traynor (Bass Place). The last named was a relative of Donnelly's while Gregson was a prominent English pugilist whose songs and poems were so popular that he was known as Bob Gregson P.P. (Poet to Pugilism).

Unfortunately, the newspapers left it to the letter writers to debate the conflicting assertions, and made no effort to ascertain the facts of a story that would make banner headlines in today's tabloids. Back then, publishers had neither the resources or, it would appear, the motivation to follow up breaking stories. Although Irish newspapers were numerous, their circulations were small. Most of the printing space was given over to European and English news and had little of purely Irish interest, apart from lists of births, marriages and deaths and accounts of robberies, duels and executions, together with notices or arrivals and departures of the packet steamers. The poorer classes, even those who could read, could not afford to buy newspapers. Admittedly, the press at the time of Donnelly's departure was more preoccupied with the death of a greater figure on the world stage. On the evening of 29 January 1820, without suffering and with no return to the sanity that had deserted him ten years earlier, King George III breathed his last. For several weeks, the papers devoted most of their columns to the momentous event and its aftermath. The United Kingdom of Great Britain and Ireland now had a new king, George IV, even if he would have to wait until July of the following year to be officially crowned.

Dan Donnelly, champion of Ireland, by George Sharples, 1819.

Nearly 200 years on, it is impossible to ascertain the facts of Donnelly's reported disinterment. It seems quite likely that the group of publicans who dismissed the story acted to save their own skins. They had been entrusted with arranging to have the grave protected. Resurrectionists, so called because they raised bodies from the dead, were extremely active in Ireland and Britain until the passing of the Second Anatomy Act of 1832, which gave licence to anatomy teachers and students to dissect donated cadavers.

Up to then, the only 'working material' allowable by law were the bodies of executed criminals. In Edinburgh, one of the main centres in the British Isles of anatomical study, there was an annual average of 850 anatomy students, yet there were only about 70 executions per year. Demand so exceeded supply that the colleges had to go outside the law to properly train their pupils, hence the need for the grave robbers. Reprehensible though their ghoulish trade undoubtedly was, the world of surgery and medicine felt it owed them a lasting debt.

Most people associate the grim business of body snatching with the evil partnership of expatriate Irishmen William Burke and William Hare. Using Edinburgh as their base, Burke, who was born in Cork, and Hare, from Derry, were murderers rather than grave robbers. They were known to have killed at least fifteen people in a twelve-month period and sold the corpses for surgical dissection. When they were eventually caught, Burke was sentenced to hanging. Hare, who turned King's evidence, received a pardon and, blinded as a result of an accident, roamed the streets of London for many years. In Dublin, it was Dan Donnelly's burial place, Bully's Acre, which was the happy hunting ground for grave robbers. There were frequent violent confrontations between Sack-'em-Ups and Dead Watchers. Many prominent professors and surgeons were in league with the perpetrators. Some paid dearly for their participation in the vile trade. The son of John Kirby, head of a prestigious school of surgery and anatomy, was caught in the act of digging up a corpse and was shot dead by a relative of the deceased.

Dr Peter Harken, an assistant to Sir Philip Crampton at his private medical school in Dawson Street, survived an assault, but paid dearly for his crime. As he tried to make his escape, he had only managed to climb on top of the outer wall when his pursuers caught hold of his legs. Harken's students, meanwhile, held onto his arms on the other side and managed to eventually win the tug-of-war. Harken never fully recovered from his injuries and his premature death a few years later was attributed to being dragged backwards and forwards across the rough wall. Christopher Dixon, a porter at the Royal College of Surgeons, was lucky to escape with his life after being caught stealing a body. An irate mob dragged him to the nearby River Liffey and repeatedly dunked him until he nearly drowned.

'Zozimus' (Michael Moran), the blind street singer who lived all of his life in the Liberties district of Dublin, had a great fear that the body snatchers would get him if he died alone in his rented room. In one of his ballads, he pleaded with his friend 'Stony Pockets':

> Oh Stony, Stony,
> Don't let the Sack-'em-Ups get me;
> Send round the hat
> And buy me a grave.

'Stony Pockets' (he got the name because he kept his right-hand pocket filled with stones to straighten up his left-tilted gait) dutifully raised enough money to ensure 'Zozimus' would be buried in the relative safety of Glasnevin Cemetery.

Body snatchers, commonly known as Sack-'em-Ups, sold their 'catches' to surgeons and anatomy teachers.

In Dan Donnelly's case, the value of his stolen corpse might have been greater as a showpiece than being carved up in anatomy classes. While the going rate for cadavers at the beginning of the nineteenth century was about two guineas (£2.2s), some fetched as much as £40, more than most people earned in a year at that time. Donnelly's fame, and his well-developed muscular structure, would have made his remains a prize catch. Perhaps he was destined

for the same fate that befell another remarkable specimen of Irish manhood, Charles Byrne (1761–83). Billed
as 'the Irish Giant', Byrne measured seven feet six inches
and made a living as a member of a travelling show. Part
of his repertoire was to light his pipe from a street gas-
lamp while standing on the ground. When John Hunter,
the renowned London surgeon and anatomist, heard that
Byrne was dying, he ordered one of his assistants to keep
watch on his house. Byrne, who had a pathological fear of
what might happen after he died, became aware of Hunter's interest and arranged for his body to be buried at sea
in a lead-weighted coffin. Hunter tracked down the under-
taker's crew and persuaded them to surrender their 'cargo'
for the remarkable sum of £500. The giant's cadaver was
smuggled into Hunter's premises, where it was shoved into
a boiler and cooked until the flesh separated easily from
the bones. Byrne's skeleton is still on show at the Royal
College of Surgeons in London.

Donnelly's body, according to stories handed down,
was traced to the premises of a prominent Dublin surgeon named Hall, who was warned he could find himself
taking the late Irish champion's place if he did not agree
to have the corpse reburied. Realizing he had no choice,
he gave in to the demand, but only returned part of the
remains. He secretly cut off the fighting hero's right arm
and, either through a prior arrangement or for fear of the
repercussions if he was found out, shipped it away to Scotland. For many years, the preserved limb was kept at Edinburgh University, where it may have been used by artists

as well as anatomical students. Usually, plaster casts were sufficient for this purpose, but actual body parts were sometimes used. A question often asked about Donnelly's arm is how can it have survived for almost 200 years? There were several ways of ensuring the preservation of anatomical specimens in the early nineteenth century. One involved the use of mercury-based chemical compounds. Another was the 'drying' procedure. This involved removing the skin and any underlying fat while leaving the muscles attached to the bone. Blood vessels were then injected with coloured waxes – red for arteries, blue for veins – and the tissue washed with an alkali solution before being air-dried. Finally, the specimen was given a coat of varnish to protect it. A third method of preservation – perhaps the most appropriate in Donnelly's case as a publican known to be 'fond of his drop' – was by immersing the body part in a tank of alcohol.

In time, Donnelly's severed arm apparently outlived its usefulness in anatomy classes and was passed on to the owner of a travelling show, who profited well for many years from his odd exhibit. In 1904, it returned to Ireland. Hugh 'Texas' McAlevey, a well-known Belfast publican, bookmaker and city councillor, put it on display in a glass case at The Duncairn Arms, in Duncairn Gardens. Eventually, McAlevey either got tired of looking at it or he feared the grisly relic was putting off customers, so he hid it away in the attic of his bookmaker's shop in Winetavern Street, Belfast. A popular cabaret artist, Bernie Small, remembered working for 'Texas' as a teenager and being warned not to go into the attic because Donnelly's ghost haunted it. On McAlevey's death, the attic was cleared out and the arm came into the possession of a Belfast wine merchant, Tom Donnelly, who was not related to the famous fighter.

In 1953, Ireland celebrated An Tostal, a national festival designed to lift the nation's spirits during a period of severe economic depression, and local organizations and individuals were encouraged to stage events to mark the occasion. Jim Byrne Junior, owner of The Hideout pub in Kilcullen, County Kildare, saw the commercial benefits of linking his premises to the legend of Dan Donnelly. The site of Dan's famous victories over English opposition on the Curragh was just two miles from the crossroads in Kilcullen where his pub was situated. Byrne arranged for a re-enactment of the Dubliner's fight with George Cooper to be staged in Donnelly's Hollow and, at the same time, he showed off his prized possession, the boxer's preserved arm, in a display case at The Hideout. The pub doubled as a mini-museum, with historic items like a landlord's crop (a reminder of the Irish land war), a pike from the 1798 rebellion, and a flag carried in Irish MP Daniel O'Connell's victory parade, all vying with Donnelly's arm for attention. A large painting of Donnelly that had been commissioned by 'Texas' McAlevey for display in his Belfast pub now adorned a wall in The Hideout. The artist, Joseph P. Carney of New York, included the stirring ballad of Donnelly and Cooper, a depiction of the monument marking the fight site, and a caption that claimed Donnelly's arms were the longest in the history of pugilism – he could button his knee-breeches without stooping! It is a pity to dismiss the myth, but Dan's preserved arm is not of abnormal length. It matches the measurement of a man of just above six feet, which Donnelly was, when using the guide of an average arm span, from fingertip to fingertip, being about the same as a person's height.

The late Jim Byrne Junior holding Donnelly's arm, which he kept on display at his pub, The Hideout, in Kilcullen, Co. Kildare. Photo courtesy M.P. Fleming.

TWO

The People's Champion

Townsend Street, in the docklands area of Dublin, was the birthplace of Dan Donnelly, probably in 1788. His birth date is undocumented, while newspaper accounts at the time of his death in 1820 varied his age from thirty-two to forty-four. The original inscription on the monument in Donnelly's Hollow on the Curragh of Kildare stated that he was born in 1770. When a new tablet was installed there, the year of his birth was changed to the more widely accepted 1788. One of the most authoritative histories of bare-knuckle boxing, *Pugilstica*, by Henry Downes Miles, published in 1866, listed him as being born in March 1788, as did Nat Fleischer's *Ring Record Book* (1962). Registration of Irish births, marriages and deaths did not commence until 1846.

Dan was the ninth of seventeen children, including four sets of twins, born during the thirty-six years his parents lived in Townsend Street. The doctor who attended his birth was allegedly so impressed by the baby's sturdy appearance that he told the proud mother: 'Mrs Donnelly, this child will one day be the wonder of his country.' The doctor's prophecy was recalled by one of Dan's sisters at the time of his death.

Whatever his potential as a 'boy wonder', Dan received no preferential treatment from his parents. Each member of the large family got an equal share of love and attention. They were tough times for the Donnellys. The eight shillings a week that Dan's father, Joseph, earned as a carpenter could not be guaranteed, as he suffered from bronchitis and was often out of work. There was no such thing then as sick pay. As a boy, Dan was said to be 'serene and composed and he bore injury with patience'. Strongly built and boisterous, he would nevertheless go to great lengths to avoid getting into fights. But this was a time of frequent pitched battles on the streets of Dublin, mainly between rival gangs on opposite sides of the River Liffey, the Liberty Boys and the Ormond Boys. Knowledge of self-defence was a considerable asset. At times Dan, forced into combat lest doubts be cast upon his courage, had to take on older, bigger boys. Many a time his mother would be required to provide words of comfort on his injured pride. School held no great attraction for young Donnelly, and his mother frequently had to abandon her heavy household chores to take the reluctant boy by the hand to his classroom on

George's Quay. Though of average intelligence, his school-ing has been described as 'irregular' and 'unfinished'.

The Donnellys were among the luckier families in an era of great hardship for the under-privileged. At least they had a part-time breadwinner. Unemployment was rife throughout Ireland because of periodic trade depres-sion, and poverty was exacerbated by high rents and low wages. 'Poverty, disease and wretchedness exist in every large town, but in Dublin the misery is indescrib-able,' wrote J.C. Curwin, former Member of Parliament for the Isle of Man, who toured Ireland shortly after the Act of Union was established in 1800. Two years earlier, Revd James Whitelaw, rector of St Catherine's Church in Thomas Street, carried out a population census of the city (he estimated it at 182,000) and was appalled at the living conditions of the poor: 'My assistants and I, undeterred by the dread of infectious diseases, undismayed by degrees of filth, stench and darkness inconceivable by those who have not experienced them, explored, in the burning summer months of 1798, every room of these wretched habitations from the cellar to the garret and on the spot ascertained their population.' A sparse single-roomed apartment rated from one to two shillings and, to ease the rent burden, two, three or four families would often share the room. Whitelaw frequently found 'from ten to sixteen persons of both sexes and all ages in a room not fifteen feet square, stretched on a wad of filthy straw, swarming with vermin and without any covering save the wretched rags that con-stituted their wearing apparel.' Not surprisingly, crime was rife. Riots and robberies were commonplace. Churches were robbed and shop windows smashed and looted. Children were snatched from their parents for the sake of their clothes and turned naked onto the streets. Better-off citizens were murdered for their rings and watches. Beggars were everywhere. The grim conditions left the population susceptible to fevers and there were frequent epidemics, the worst being from 1817 to 1819. However, for those on the other end of the scale – the rich – Dublin was an attractive, popular city that boasted a brilliant social life. Little did young Dan Donnelly realize that he would experience both extremes during his short lifetime.

For all his giddiness and lack of application to any given task, Dan had his compensatory qualities. He was never known to bear a lasting grudge against anyone, even those who got the better of him in street scraps, and he was considerate to the needs of his poorer playmates. His mother would readily answer his pleas for bread to satisfy his hungry pals. She made the small sacrifice gladly. If Dan's early aversion to discipline and well-meant advice was to remain a characteristic into adulthood, so was his sense of compassion. At the height of his fame, he would never leave the scene of a fight until he had consoled his beaten opponent and checked his condition.

This most admirable trait was inherited from his grandfather, Daniel Donnelly, whose kindness was renowned far beyond the County Louth parish of Cooley, where he had a well-cultivated farm adequately stocked with cattle. Shelter for the orphan, the poor, and the travelling stranger were never refused at the Donnelly farm. Old Daniel made sure his five sons got a good education and brought them up 'in the best traditions of charity, humility and true Christianity'. When he died at a ripe old age, he was widely grieved. The farm passed into the hands of his two eldest sons, Hugh and James. They were not as successful at the task as their father had been and it looked like the family might have to find other means of survival. One of the boys, Joseph, later to become father of the famed prizefighter, accepted an offer to travel to Newry, County Down, and learn the carpentry trade from a Scot, Arthur McDonald, an old friend of the family. It was while he was living there that Joseph married a member of the high-ranking Gore family. The couple moved a few miles south to Dundalk, where they set up home and Joseph went to work at his newly learned trade. A plea from his aged, widowed mother persuaded him to return to the family farm until she died. Joseph and his wife then packed their meagre belongings and journeyed to Dublin, where they spent the rest of their days.

Townsend Street, where they settled, got its name literally from being the street at the end of the town. Up to the middle of the seventeenth century, the River Liffey had remained unwalled and the sea came right up to where the street now meets Lombard Street. From 1792 up to the early 1900s, it was the location of the Westmoreland (or Lock) Hospital, established for 'indiscriminate admission of all indigent persons' and the treatment of sexually transmitted diseases. Donnelly may well have found its services useful after returning home from England, where he picked up a venereal disease while supposedly dedicating himself to training for a fight with Tom Oliver.

Dublin city centre in 1820, the year of Donnelly's death. The view is from Carlisle Bridge, later replaced by O'Connell Bridge.

As a youth, Dan found hurling, handball and other sporting pursuits more deserving of his energy and time than carpentry, the trade into which he followed his father on leaving school at the age of twelve. It did not take much persuasion from his out-of-work pals to make him give the job a miss for a day or two. Many a lecture he got from his despairing parents for his carelessness. One of Dan's workmates at Connery's timber yard in Sir John Robertson's Quay, where he served his apprenticeship, was Arthur Devlin, brother of Robert Emmet's housekeeper, Anne Devlin. Donnelly's patriotic spirit was fanned by his friendship with Arthur, who, along with the rest of his family, was jailed for his part in the abortive uprising led by Emmet in 1803. In his more serious moments, Dan would speak proudly of his love for Ireland and of how he despised those who turned their backs on their country.

Most of the time, however, he was as cheerful a companion as anyone could wish for. There was rarely a dull moment with Dan. He was a great storyteller and was always ready to burst into song, dance a jig or go on a drinking spree with his mates. His cheerful disposition was, when he attained his fame, to make him one of the most sought-after escorts in Ireland. Although he had a reputation of being handy with his fists when the need arose, he was, in reality, quite a mild-mannered youth. Almost impossible to provoke, he would go to great lengths to avoid settling an argument in the traditional Irish manner.

One thing that was guaranteed to upset him was to see the old, the feeble or the under-privileged mistreated in any way. Then, it was said, 'No lion could display more fury.' Once he heard of an old, poverty-stricken neighbour in Townsend Street who had died alone with no one to claim her remains. The woman's death was attributed to a highly contagious fever and people stayed away for fear of catching the disease. Donnelly was determined that she should get a decent burial and asked for help in removing the body. Finding no volunteers, Dan went alone to the dark, dingy tenement room, tied a rope around the crude coffin and hoisted it onto his back for transfer to a local churchyard. A church sexton who was busy levelling the bottom of a newly dug grave was startled by the shadow of the brawny youth suddenly appearing. Donnelly told him he wished to bury the woman there, but was firmly told that the grave was reserved for 'a person of distinction'. Dan eyed the sexton sternly and, controlling his temper, told him: 'If you don't stand aside, it is you who will be occupying this grave. This is a land of equality and this woman has as much right to be buried here as anyone.' He met no further resistance as he lowered the coffin, took the sexton's shovel and completed the burial.

On another occasion, Donnelly's role of Good Samaritan almost cost him his life, or at least might have prevented him ever earning fame in the prize ring. Late one night, on his way home from a pub in Ringsend, he heard the terrified screams of a young woman. Though feeling somewhat giddy after several hours' drinking, he traced the distress call to a dark alley, where the woman was struggling desperately with two attackers. They dragged her to the dockside and tossed her into the Liffey. Without hesitation, Dan slipped off his jacket, plunged into the cold, murky waters and swam some twenty yards to where the woman struggled to stay afloat. Although she almost slipped out of his grasp, the gallant rescuer managed to get her ashore, only to find the ruffians waiting to turn their wrath upon him. Too exhausted to put up much of a fight, Dan was viciously punched, kicked and beaten with a stone until he was left barely conscious. A couple of passers-by took him to hospital, where the attending physician shook his head on discovering that the hero's arm was broken in four places. 'I am sorry,' he told Dan's distraught parents, who had been summoned to the hospital, 'but this arm will have to be amputated.' They pleaded with him to try and save the limb. Dr Abraham Colles, a man whose compassion and care for the city's poor was widely acknowledged, was so impressed with what he was told of the young man's charitable acts that he promised to do what he could. With infinite patience and delicate skill, he pieced together the shattered bones until, his job successfully done, he placed his arm around Dan's shoulders and proclaimed him 'a pocket Hercules'.

So another underprivileged Dublin family, the Donnellys, had cause to bestow their blessings on the much-loved Dr Colles. The Kilkenny-born medic came from a long line of surgeons and was twice president of the Royal College of Surgeons in Dublin. After being conferred MD in Edinburgh, he spent some time in London before returning to Dublin to teach anatomy and surgery at his rented rooms in South King Street. He was later appointed to the Dispensary for the Sick Poor in Meath Street and was district visitor for the Sick and Indigent Roomkeepers' Society. A contemporary credited Dr Colles with 'solid judgement, manly directness, perfect probity, the soundest of understandings and the kindest of hearts'. Widely acclaimed as a medical researcher and graphic lecturer, one of his papers on the fracture of a forearm bone was so highly considered that the term *Colles fracture* is still used all over the world.

THREE

Beating a Bully

Like many famous boxers in history, Donnelly discovered, more by accident than design, that he had the basic requirements of strength, courage and skill to equip himself in the ring by being reluctantly drawn into battle with a bully. Then in his early twenties, he was enjoying a quiet, after-work drink with his ailing father when Joseph Donnelly took a sudden fit of violent coughing. A burly sailor, who had just come ashore, verbally abused the stricken man. Dan implored him to show some respect, which earned a curt retort from the sailor: 'Any cheek from you, me young bucko, and I'll teach you a lesson in respect.'

Dan controlled his temper and pleaded that they be left in peace, but the tormentor persisted with his tirade until Donnelly, his patience finally exhausted, said: 'I have no desire to fight you, but if it's what you want, then I'll not back down.' The sailor placed his glass on the bar counter, wiped his mouth with his tattooed forearm and rushed at Donnelly. The young man stood his ground and met the charge with a terrific right-hand punch to the aggressor's face. The counter shook under the impact of the big man as he landed, blood pouring from his nose. Resuming his attack, he fought with Dan for fully fifteen minutes until the chastened sailor slumped to the sawdust-covered floor, gasping 'enough' through his bloody, swollen lips.

The news of how Donnelly had tamed the bully spread swiftly through the neighbourhood. At every local bar he visited for several weeks afterwards, he was toasted as a hero. One man who did not share the general adoration was a local who had done some boxing and called himself the district champion. He threw out a challenge to Donnelly to prove who was the better man. Dan would not hear of it. 'I have no wish to be classed as a fighting man,' he repeatedly told those who asked would he accept the challenge. It was only when doubts were cast on his courage that he yielded to the pressure. The match was arranged and Donnelly beat his rival so severely that the loser expressed the parting hope that they would never meet again. It is not recorded where the fight took place, but boxing and wrestling bouts were frequently held in fields behind St Mark's church, close to Dan's home, and attracted large crowds.

All of Dublin heard of about the fighting ability of the hero from Townsend Street, but he politely declined the numerous challenges. An experienced fighter generally recognized as the city champion sought out Donnelly, following him to his favourite drinking haunts and repeatedly demanding a showdown. Dan stuck to his expressed desire for a quiet life, until the occasion when his pursuer called him a coward before his friends. He agreed to a match, which was arranged for six days later on the banks of the Grand Canal. Word of the contest aroused considerable excitement throughout the city, and a fair-sized crowd gathered to witness the bare-knuckle encounter. Small wagers were laid on the result. Right up to the time the contestants stripped off for action, Donnelly continued trying to talk his rival out of fighting. His pleas were in vain.

In the early rounds, Dan's reluctance to get engaged drew disparaging comments from the audience. He fought mainly on the retreat, trying to block or avoid his opponent's heavy blows. Only when he saw the encounter was likely to be prolonged did he become more aggressive. He gradually gained the upper hand and, in a furious attack in the sixteenth round, he sent the other man sprawling to the ground. Defeat was conceded and Donnelly was proclaimed the new champion of Dublin. There were no further challenges, which pleased him no end.

Around this time, a conversation took place in an English tavern between two pugilists and two members of The Fancy, as dedicated followers of sports like boxing were known. The fighters poured scorn on Ireland's reputation as a nation of courageous men. They said they had gone there and issued open challenges to the best pugilists the

*Captain William Kelly, Donnelly's patron, was a talented
performer on the uilleann pipes, which he played before George IV
on the monarch's visit to Ireland in 1821. From a painting owned
by Kelly's granddaughter, Mrs Bailie.*

country could produce, but had found no acceptors. One of the men engaged in the discussion was Captain William Kelly, owner of a prominent horse-racing establishment in Maddenstown, County Kildare. A keen follower of boxing, he was stung at the affront to his fellow countrymen and resolved to find a fighting Irishman who would disprove the English fighters' slur. His companion, a Scotsman named Robert Barclay Allardice, better known as Captain Barclay, agreed to help Kelly in his quest.

The pair travelled to Dublin, where they were told of the promise shown by Dan Donnelly. They were warned, however, that they would have quite a job persuading him to enter the ring. Sure enough, on meeting Kelly and Barclay, the amiable carpenter showed no enthusiasm for their stated plans. 'I am sorry if I have wasted your time, gentlemen,' he informed them, 'but I am a man of peace.' Kelly, the jibes of the Englishmen still ringing in his ears, was not ready to admit defeat. He used every possible ploy in his efforts to get Donnelly to change his mind. He recalled stirring tales of ancient Irish heroes shedding their blood in defence of their country's honour. He told Dan of how much his nation would be indebted to him if he could ridicule the foreigners' claims. Besides, Kelly concluded, there was good money to be made from the ring.

Dan was silent for a few minutes, and then informed Kelly he would think over his offer and give his decision in a few days. On their return, he gave what appeared to be a well-rehearsed speech: 'Gentlemen, I shall first return to you my sincere thanks for the great dependence you have on my fidelity towards my country. The honour you have bestowed on me shall ever be cherished in my bosom. To appear before a multitude of spectators on a plain is wholly against my will, yet my country claims my support.' Holding up his right fist, he vowed: 'I owe no spleen to Great Britain, but the man of any nation who presumes to offer an insult to my country, this arm, while my life blood flows, shall defy.'

Robert Barclay Allardice, better known as 'Captain Barclay',
parliamentarian and renowned long-distance walker, trained
many prominent pugilists, including Dan Donnelly. Courtesy Scottish
National Portrait Gallery.

Delighted, if somewhat taken aback at the eloquence of his statement, Kelly and Barclay promised Dan he would receive the full benefit of their experience and teaching. Several other versions of how Donnelly was 'discovered' have been handed down, one claiming that Kelly had, quite by accident, watched Dan demolishing a bar-full of men with a single blow to each, and was so impressed that he signed up the brawny young man on the spot. The most fanciful of all the accounts, undoubtedly, was that told by Malachi Horan, the wonderful old storyteller from Killenarden, County Wicklow. Dr George A. Little, one-time president of the Old Dublin Society, recorded Horan's colourful yarns and had them published in a book, *Malachi Horan Remembers*. The story about Donnelly, for all its improbabilities, is related in Malachi's quaint, colourful style:

> Dan Donnelly was a hedge carpenter, out of Dublin. He was a big, loose man, like a reaping hook. He travelled this road and every road looking for work. One day and him passing Captain Kelly's of Valleymount [the story-teller is misquoted here; he obviously referred to Ballymount, County Kildare, not Valleymount, County Wicklow] he looked over the fence and saw the captain and him taking a beating from a rough-looking martyr. Captain Kelly was a great man for the boxing; he had half the country fighting. After him watching a bit, Donnelly could stand it no longer. He ups and shouts to the Captain: 'Eh, man, will you go in and fight and stop waiting to be beat.' That seemed to freshen up the Captain, for he downed his man. All over, he came up

to Donnelly and asked him would he have a fancy to try his hand. Donnelly, who saw his dinner in it, took the chance quick enough.

Boys-o-boys, that was the sore day in Valleymount. It was like ninepins the way Dan knocked down every man put up to him by Captain Kelly. It was not only his dinner that Donnelly got on the head of it; no, indeed, for the Captain hired him to work about the place. Of course, the fighting was Captain Kelly's object, for he was the great trainer. The Captain near burst with interest teaching Donnelly, but not a mite more than his sister, Miss Kelly. Clean crazy she was about Donnelly's fighting. And Dan repaid them very well. As sure as there is tinkers in Wicklow, he had every man in the country beat before they knew he was in it. And not a hair out of Donnelly either. Soon there was nothing left for him to beat.

Malachi Horan, born in 1847, at the time of the Great Famine, deplored the fact that Donnelly was not around in the same period as Simon Byrne, a renowned Irish pugilist who fought between 1825 and 1833. 'Gor-a-wor, but that would have been a match,' enthused the storyteller. 'A quiet, easy-going lad was Simon, but tough as a furze and clean as a whip. Ah, it is the pity of the world that he never fought Dan Donnelly.' (Simon Byrne was so badly beaten by James 'Deaf' Burke in a brutal battle lasting three hours and sixteen minutes that he died from his injuries.)

Captain Kelly installed Donnelly at his brother's residence in Calverstown, near the Curragh of Kildare. There he was taught the rudiments of boxing skill and the means of achieving physical fitness by Kelly's friend, Captain Barclay. He could not have been in better hands. Barclay, a patron of two of the greatest bare-knuckle champions of England, John Gully and Tom Cribb, was acknowledged as one of the foremost trainers of his era. His renown stretched beyond the boxing ring. Member of Parliament for the County of Kincardine for three successive terms, he was a close friend of William Pitt 'the Younger', the prime minister who effected the Union of Great Britain and Ireland in 1800. Barclay also claimed the title of Earl of Monteith and Airth. Over six feet tall, handsome and well built, Barclay was an acclaimed athlete and often sparred with the fighters he trained. His strength enabled him, according to legend, to lift a man of eighteen stone from floor to tabletop with one hand. As a long-distance walker, he won many wagers on his accomplishments. On one occasion he covered the 510 miles from London to Ury in ten days and was also credited with walking eighty-one miles in under sixteen hours. Barclay was seventy-five when he died in 1854 after being kicked in the head by a horse.

Donnelly, while training under Barclay, earned his keep by looking after the cows at Calverstown Demesne. Up to the middle of the last century, the high-walled building that had been his training quarters was used as a hen run. It was roofless and in a bad state of repair when the then owner, P.J. McCall, had it demolished and replaced with stables. Donnelly's initials were supposed to have been carved on rafters at Calverstown House, but there is no trace of them today. They were probably in the old buildings that were pulled down after McCall purchased the estate from Otway Freeman in 1958 for use as a stud farm. McCall could recall a pair of large dumb-bells lying about the place when he took it over. They were almost certainly part of Donnelly's training equipment, but they were badly affected by wood-worm and were disposed of for that reason.

Whatever the value of his association with Captain Barclay, it is not so certain that he did well to come under the patronage of Captain William Kelly. He came from a family of noted eccentrics, popularly known as 'the mad Kellys of Maddenstown'. They had some odd ways of entertaining themselves, such as 'dancing in their pelts'. Captain Kelly, a dedicated gambler, would wager on bouts of arm wrestling and on which of two flies left a wall first. Kelly lived at Maddenstown House, in County Kildare, and the property had fallen into ruin by the time P.J. Prendergast, the renowned racehorse trainer and bloodstock breeder, took it over. For many years before it was demolished, the building was known locally as 'Cooper's ruins' in remembrance of the battered state of George Cooper after the Englishman was defeated by Donnelly in their epic battle on the Curragh.

Kelly, as well as being a successful horse breeder, enjoyed some fame as a musician. A talented performer on the uilleann pipes, he performed before King George IV on the occasion of the monarch's visit to Ireland in 1821, using a set of pipes presented to him by the same personage when he was Prince of Wales. The magnificent ebony pipes, tipped with ivory and with silver-plated mountings and engraved 'William Kelly, esq., 1809' were on display at Kilkea Castle, Castledermot, County Kildare, for many years, but their current whereabouts are unknown. The castle, an 1849 reconstruction of a medieval structure associated with Gerald, the famous 'Wizard' (eleventh) Earl of Kildare, was the seat of the Fitzgeralds, Dukes of Leinster, before being turned into an hotel.

A measure of Kelly's ability to pass on his musical talents is borne out by the international fame earned by some of his pupils. Among them was the renowned 'Kildare Piper' Johnny Hicks, whose performances on the pipes delighted audiences in Britain and the United States as well as in his own country. Captain Francis O'Neill, in his book *Irish Minstrels and Musicians*, said of Kelly: 'If we are to judge the teacher by the style and execution of those who graduated under his tuition, the renowned turfman must be ranked among the best pipers of the day.' Because of his affection for the pipes, Kelly named several of his horses after parts of the instrument, such as Drone, Chanter and Bellows. A particularly fine grey horse was Drone and his successes are recorded in the racing calendars of the period. Kelly retained his 'Captain' title from his time serving with the British Army. Two of his brothers also achieved ranking positions in the force. Colonel Ponsonby Kelly commanded the 24th Regiment, while Captain Waldron Kelly served in the 41st Regiment. Their cousin, Colonel Edward Kelly, was said to have 'performed brilliant service on the field at Waterloo'.

Captain William Kelly, Donnelly's backer, was born at New Abbey House in County Kildare around the year 1780. He married his cousin, Catherine Orford, of Rathbride Manor, and they had seven sons and one daughter. After a long and distinguished career on the turf, he retired to his Dublin townhouse in Marino Crescent, where he died around 1858. A young neighbour of his was Bram Stoker, who went on to become a civil servant before turning to writing the classic horror novel *Dracula*. Stoker later served as secretary to Sir Henry Irving, the acknowledged 'king' of Victorian melodrama, and managed Irving's London theatre, the Lyceum.

If Captain Kelly's love of Ireland helped boost Dan Donnelly's nationalistic spirit, it is equally certain that his fondness for the 'wild life' rubbed off on the impressionable pugilist. It did not take much encouragement from his friends to skip training and join them in the numerous taverns close to his temporary abode. Nevertheless, he responded to Kelly's advice and knuckled down to serious training under Captain Barclay.

His first major test as a prizefighter was about to take place. Tom Hall, a prominent English pugilist, was on a tour of Ireland giving sparring exhibitions and instructing young boxers. When he was approached to fight Donnelly, he accepted without hesitation. He had never heard of the Irishman and saw the contest as a way of earning easy money.

The match was set for the Curragh of Kildare on 14 September 1814. The 100-guinea purse would be split, sixty for the winner and forty for the loser. Many of Donnelly's friends had serious misgivings about the encounter. They thought Dan was being too severely tested in his first ring outing under the patronage of Captain Kelly. Hall, from the Isle of Wight, was three years younger than the Dubliner, but was considerably more experienced. He had been described as 'the most courageous pugilist in England' and numbered among his victims George Cribb, brother of the legendary Tom Cribb, former champion of England.

Donnelly's advice to those who doubted his chances was to be sensible: 'Don't bet on me, then you won't lose too much if I am beaten.' However, the possibility of defeat did not really enter his mind, and to those who were prepared to wager heavily on his success, he boasted that he would 'rather die than yield to Tom Hall'. Indeed, so cocksure was he that he felt it unnecessary to stick to the rigid training programme set out by Captain Barclay. Part of that regimen was early-morning walks through the fields around Calverstown before returning to his training quarters for breakfast. Many a time, Dan would fail to show up for his morning meal. Search parties would eventually track him down to a village tavern where his growing band of supporters was plying him with alcoholic drinks. Bad enough for someone with an empty stomach, but disastrous for an athlete in training. Captain Kelly set up a wide network of spies to make sure his protégé was kept well away from the dens of temptation and Dan seemed to be in remarkably good condition on the day of the fight.

FOUR

King of the Curragh

All roads to the Curragh on the morning of 14 September 1814 were jammed with coaches, jaunting cars, gigs, carts and drays, men on horseback, and those who had no means of transport. If many had to walk the thirty miles from Dublin, would it not be worth it to see the big fight, and to be able to tell their grandchildren they were there on the day Dan Donnelly conquered Tom Hall? Black-shawled widows gripped the hands of their bare-footed offspring as they hurried along, chattering excitedly with their fellow pedestrians. It helped relieve the monotony of the long journey.

By one o'clock in the afternoon, when the contest was due to begin, an estimated 20,000 people filled every inch of the hollow, at the base of which a twenty-two-foot square had been roped off. The hillsides formed a natural amphitheatre, ensuring a decent view of the ring for all those in attendance. The spot was known as Belcher's Hollow, after Englishman Tom Belcher's victory there over an Irishman named Dougherty the previous year. On this day, however, it would be re-named Donnelly's Hollow, and so it remains.

The extraordinary interest generated by the fight between Donnelly and Hall was primarily down to word-of-mouth publicity. Dan's reputation as a fighting man of outstanding quality might have been exaggerated, but he would acquire the status of a hero if he could beat down his English opponent. It was a time, too, when the public had a fondness for brutal, blood-letting spectacles, and pugilism fitted in neatly alongside such 'sports' as cock-fighting, bull-baiting and dog fights. Public executions were guaranteed to draw huge audiences. Bare-knuckle prizefights contained enough savagery and shows of blood to satisfy the most sadistic taste. Unlike modern boxing, where heavily padded gloves provide at least some protection for the face, as well as the hands, which are also wrapped in bandages, bare-fist battles would often result in severe damage to both victor and vanquished. Broken fingers, torn muscles and sprained wrists were as common as fractured noses, broken ribs and concussion. Blows to the eyes, the side of the neck and the throat were considered especially effective. In Daniel Mendoza's *The Modern Art of Boxing*, published in 1789, the English champion described one of the most telling punches that delivered 'under the short

Dan Donnelly stood six foot and half an inch, and weighed fourteen stone. His main attributes were his strength, stamina and courage. New York Clipper, *5 September 1857.*

ribs or in the kidneys, as it is termed, which deprives the person struck of his breath, occasions an instant discharge of urine, puts him in the greatest torture and renders him for some time a cripple'.

All bare-fist battles were fought to the finish, only ending when one of the contestants was beaten unconscious or conceded defeat, or if nightfall or the intervention of the police caused a halt to the proceedings. Rounds were of indeterminate duration, lasting until one or both of the fighters fell to the ground. After thirty seconds' rest, the men were required to answer the call of 'Time'. Failure to appear at the 'scratch line' drawn in the centre of the ring would be taken as acceptance of defeat. So if one reads of a bare-knuckle fight lasting for fifty rounds or more, the actual amount of time spent in combat could be a lot less than a modern twelve-round bout of fixed three-minute rounds. Some of the old prizefights lasted only a few min-utes while others dragged on for hours. It was common practice for a tired participant to touch down on one knee so he could avail of the half-minute break. Ring battles could be vicious, with nothing to stop a contestant bash-ing his rival's head against a wooden corner-post, elbowing him in the face, or getting a stranglehold around his neck with one arm while belting him with his free hand. Pugil-ists like Dan Donnelly fought under the Rules of Boxing drawn up by former English champion Jack Broughton in 1743, which did not forbid butting, eye-gouging, hair-pulling, or wrestling. It was not until 1853, thirty-three years after Donnelly's death, that the Broughton code was replaced by the London Prize Ring Rules. The introduction of gloves came with the Marquis of Queensberry Rules in 1867. Though there have been some modifications down through the years, the Queensberry Rules still apply.

First to enter the ring, to thunderous applause, Donnelly looked the picture of fitness and confidence. So focussed was he on the job ahead that he barely noticed the slaps on his back and shouts of 'Good luck, Dan' from excited fans. Hall followed a few minutes later and threw his hat into the ring, signifying his readiness to do battle. He ducked through the ropes, walked straight up to Donnelly and shook his hand. Bowing respectfully to the assembly, he addressed them with a well-prepared speech. 'Gentlemen of Ireland,' he began, 'I come here not to shed contempt on your country; if I did I would not consider myself worthy of calling myself a man.' The hushed crowd heard him continue: 'England is the place of my birth, and nature has designed me to gain a living by the power of my arm. My profession, therefore, is that of a pugilist, to whom all countries are alike. The man of any nation who professes the same character is the man for me. Therefore, I hope your hospitable hearts will not be moved to envy me, as the stranger who now has the honour of standing before you means not to degrade the land of Erin, but to try his strength with a man.'

Loud applause greeted his eloquent address. The contestants then 'took a glass together' before stripping off. It was plain that the Irishman held all of the physical advantages. Measuring half an inch over six feet and weighing around fourteen stone, he was three inches taller and over two stone heavier than Hall, who would be categorized as a super-middleweight in modern boxing. Donnelly was seconded by the 'two captains', Kelly and Barclay, while two prominent English pugilists, Jack Carter and Ned Painter, were in the visitor's corner. Despite his smaller stature, the betting odds favoured Hall by six to four on. It was generally thought that his wider experience and superior skill would make him too much of a handful for the raw Dubliner.

A newspaper account noted that 'several very respectable females were seated among the crowd', evidence of Dan's sex appeal. 'Gorgeous' Georges Carpentier is generally credited with being the first famous boxer to set womanly hearts a-flutter, and their presence at the Frenchman's challenge for Jack Dempsey's world heavyweight title in 1921 helped generate the sport's first million-dollar gate. Other handsome hunks that had large feminine fan clubs in the period between the two world wars included Max Baer, Len Harvey and Ireland's 'Gorgeous Gael' Jack Doyle. But Donnelly, way back in the first decade of the nineteenth century, could certainly turn female heads with his rugged good looks, his powerful physique, and his charming personality. Nor was he slow to cash in whenever the opportunity presented itself.

It was one o'clock in the afternoon when Donnelly and Hall shook hands in the centre of the ring and 'Time' was called for the contest to commence. 'A solemn silence prevailed,' one newspaper reported. Immediately, the difference in styles between the contestants was pronounced.

Donnelly's straight-up, unvarying stance contrasted with Hall's lower posture and greater flexibility in his moves. They opened cautiously, their eyes fixed steadfastly on each other. Dan attempted the first hit, a left that was blocked by his opponent's tight guard. Hall tried to counter, but missed. They fell into a clinch. Several punches were exchanged before Hall fell to the turf to end the first round, which had lasted one minute.

The second round saw Hall beating a hasty retreat as he sought to frustrate the slower Irishman and lure him into leaving his defence open. His tactics paid off. After ducking a ponderous right swing, he landed a heavy blow that split Donnelly's lip. It was 'first blood' to the visitor and first bets were settled. Dan, his pride hurt as much as his person, became more aggressive and forced Hall down. The pattern for the next three rounds was similar, Hall on the run while Donnelly plodded forward, trying to land his haymakers. Each round ended with the Englishman going down. Hall, realizing that he had to take the initiative if he was to win, surprised Donnelly by standing still and trading punches in the sixth round. Dan was beaten back and would have fallen had the ropes not supported him. Still, it was Donnelly who was on top as the round ended, with Hall once again dropping to the ground. Both men went down in a tangle in the seventh, and Dan showed signs of losing his temper in the next when Hall touched down without being struck. Donnelly drew back his foot as if to kick his kneeling rival, but was restrained by Captain Kelly, who yelled: 'Are you mad, Dan? Do you want to lose the fight?'

RULES

TO BE OBSERVED IN ALL BATTLES ON THE STAGE

I. THAT a fquare of a Yard be chalked in the middle of the Stage; and on every frefh fet-to after a fall, or being parted from the rails, each Second is to bring his Man to the fide of the fquare, and place him oppofite to the other, and till they are fairly fet-to at the Lines, it fhall not be lawful for one to ftrike at the other.

II. That, in order to prevent any Difputes, the time a Man lies after a fall, if the Second does not bring his Man to the fide of the fquare, within the fpace of half a minute, he fhall be deemed a beaten Man.

III. That in every main Battle, no perfon whatever fhall be upon the Stage, except the Principals and their Seconds; the fame rule to be obferved in bye-battles, except that in the latter, Mr. Broughton is allowed to be upon the Stage to keep decorum, and to affift Gentlemen in getting to their places, provided always he does not interfere in the Battle; and whoever pretends to infringe thefe Rules to be turned immediately out of the houfe. Every body is to quit the Stage as foon as the Champions are ftripped, before the fet-to.

IV. That no Champion be deemed beaten, unlefs he fails coming up to the line in the limited time, or that his own Second declares him beaten. No Second is to be allowed to afk his man's Adversary any queftions, or advife him to give out.

V. That in bye-battles, the winning man to have two-thirds of the Money given, which fhall be publicly divided upon the Stage, notwithftanding any private agreements to the contrary.

VI. That to prevent Difputes, in every main Battle the Principals fhall, on coming on the Stage, choofe from among the gentlemen prefent two Umpires, who fhall abfolutely decide all Difputes that may arife about the Battle; and if the two Umpires cannot agree, the faid Umpires to choofe a third, who is to determine it.

VII. That no perfon is to hit his Adverfary when he is down, or feize him by the ham, the breeches, or any part below the waift: a man on his knees to be reckoned down.

As agreed by feveral Gentlemen at Broughton's Amphitheatre,
Tottenham Court Road, Auguft 16, 1743.

The rules of boxing drawn up by Jack Broughton in 1743 stood for almost a century until replaced by the London Prize Ring Rules.

To the delight of the Irish supporters and the consternation of the English side, it was clear that Donnelly was heading for victory. He dropped Hall with heavy rights to the head in the ninth and tenth rounds and, in the next, a left-hander had the visitor looking pained and dejected as he knelt on the turf. Hall rallied gamely in the twelfth, but the effort took too much out of him and once again he was forced down. Twice more, Hall was floored to end the subsequent rounds. The fifteenth saw the fight come to an unsatisfactory climax, with both fighters claiming the other should be disqualified.

Donnelly loaded up and let fly with a tremendous right-hander. It just missed its target, but Hall sank to the ground, as he had done several times during the contest, to gain the thirty-second rest that followed a knockdown. Dan, his patience finally exhausted, lashed out with a right that caught the sitting Englishman on the side of the head and brought blood streaming from his ear. It was a clear foul, and Hall's seconds immediately jumped into the ring, demanding that he be declared the winner. Donnelly's cornermen argued that Hall was well beaten and deserved to lose for going down so often without being hit. Besides, they insisted, the punch that Dan landed on his fallen opponent was accidental. Hall's seconds refused to let him continue. So ended, in bitter dispute, Donnelly's eagerly anticipated first major test in the prize ring.

The neutrals in attendance suggested that a draw would be the fairest result and the purse money should be split down the middle, or a rematch arranged. It was decided to leave the final decision to 'the noblemen and gentlemen of the Irish Turf Club'. A letter published in *Carrick's Morning Post* eight days after the fight said the Turf Club had decided that 'bets depending on the match between Donnelly and Hall be withdrawn and the purse should be divided between the contestants, both having deviated from the technical line of fair play'. It added that Donnelly would fight Jack Carter, one of Hall's seconds, at the Curragh during April. Two days later, in the same paper, a letter signed 'An Amateur' stated that nothing had been decided about the outcome of the fight and it had been agreed to refer the matter to the Pugilistic Club in London. The correspondent added that rumours of a match between Donnelly and Carter were unfounded. Regrettably, the newspapers failed to follow up the story and there is no record of a definitive decision on the result of the fight. Pierce Egan reported in *Boxiana* that 'the most independent and candid opinion upon the subject, from the best judges of pugilism who witnessed the battle, appears to be that BOTH of the combatants lost it'.

Exasperated by his opponent constantly going down to gain a rest, Donnelly strikes Tom Hall while he is on his knees. The fight ends in dispute, with both sides claiming victory. Famous Fights, *3 June 1901.*

*Donnelly's Hollow, pictured on a postcard sent from Kildare to London,
dated 21 September 1907.*

Whatever the claims and counter-claims, there was
no doubt in the minds of Donnelly's supporters as to who
won the battle. Every village within miles of the fight venue
enjoyed wild celebrations as news spread of the Irishman's
'victory'. Farmers' boys who had saved for six months to
buy new suits were left penniless after lengthy drinking sessions. Bonfires were lit on hillsides and people sang and
danced around them until the last embers grew cold.

As for the 'conquering hero' himself, it was fully eight
days before he was able to tear himself away from his still
jubilant supporters. He pleaded that he wished to return
to Dublin to be with his mother, now a widow, and his
brothers and sisters. No sooner had he arrived home in
Townsend Street but a huge crowd carried him off for
further celebrations at a local tavern. Dan sang, danced

and told and re-told his version of the fight until the party ended the following morning. After a few days' much-needed rest, he went back to work in the carpenter's shop. He needed the money, for he had not a single penny to show from his fight purse.

FIVE

Cooper's Challenge

On 18 June 1815, near the village of Waterloo, eight miles south of Brussels, Napoleon's French forces were defeated in battle by a combined force of British, German, Dutch and Belgian soldiers led by the Duke of Wellington. Unlike 'The Iron Duke', who famously retorted, on being reminded of his Dublin birth, that 'being born in a stable did not make one a horse', Dan Donnelly was immensely proud of his city and his country. It was in the same month as Wellington's great victory that Donnelly began forming his own plans for battle, albeit on a somewhat lesser scale than the Waterloo encounter.

Dan was working at his carpentry bench when he received word that two gentlemen wished to meet him in a local tavern. He entered the premises, ordered a pint of porter, and stood by the counter until the strangers approached him. One of them, a black American, spoke first. 'Sir, I perceive you are Mr Donnelly,' he ventured. When Dan confirmed his identity, the visitor introduced himself and his companion and told him of the reason for their call: 'This is George Cooper and I am Tom Molineaux. We are in Ireland on an exhibition tour and to teach the art of boxing. We have been told that you are the best man in Ireland and I would like to challenge you to a match.' Dan did not answer right away. While feeling honoured that two such illustrious prizefighters had sought him out, he believed there would be little glory to be gained in defeating Molineaux, who had only recently been beaten by the other man present, Cooper.

'No, I do not wish to fight a conquered man,' he declared, 'but I am willing to meet Mr Cooper if he so desires.' Another version had Donnelly refusing Molineaux because he was 'a coloured man'. Whichever is correct, Molineaux was stung at the curt dismissal of his challenge and began to hurl abuse at the Irish champion. He was calmed by Cooper, who smilingly shook Dan by the hand and said he would be happy to fight him. A sad postscript to the meeting of the three pugilists was how Molineaux, already a heavy drinker, sank steadily into decline. He was taken ill while touring the west of Ireland with a boxing show in 1818 and died of liver failure in the barrack rooms of the 77th Infantry Regiment, where some black soldiers of his acquaintance had provided him with shelter. He was thirty-four years old. It was a particularly sad ending for a man who, born into slavery on a Virginia plantation, had the effrontery to twice challenge Tom Cribb for the championship of England, only to suffer defeat on both occasions.

Tom Molineaux, a freed American slave, was one of the first black boxers to achieve fame. After his challenge to Donnelly was rejected, he went downhill and was buried in a pauper's grave in Galway. From a coloured print by W.E. Downing after an etching by Richard Dighton.

Donnelly's supporters were delighted to hear the news of his planned meeting with Cooper. The Irish champion, however, privately admitted to some misgivings. Cooper had a formidable reputation and his renowned scientific ability would be hard to combat. A native of Stone, in Staffordshire, Cooper was tagged 'the Bargeman' because he worked as a labourer on canal barges. Of a gypsy background, he was said to be the person on whom George Borrow based his boxing character 'the Flaming Tinman' in *Lavengro* and *The Romany Rye*. Rated one of the most complete prizefighters of his time, Cooper could hit hard with both hands, was noted for his skilful use of the 'one, two', was adept at blocking and countering, and topped all that with a great degree of courage. Bill Richmond, the black American pugilist who settled in England, called him 'the best natural fighter I have ever worked with'.

If there was one flaw in Cooper's fighting make-up, it was his aversion to training. This could hardly be considered advantageous to Donnelly, whose own preparation for a fight, according to one writer, 'appears to have consisted of limiting himself to twenty-five glasses of whiskey a day'. However exaggerated the comment might have been, it was certainly true that the tavern held more appeal than the training camp to the devil-may-care Irishman.

Boredom with the routine of training and the long, lonely walks that Captain Barclay prescribed led Dan to make regular stops at the pubs along the route. Captain Kelly made sure his wealthy Kildare friends took the easily led champion into their homes to be fed and entertained. They were made well aware that too close contact with the adoring peasantry would be fatal to his chances of success against Cooper.

George Cooper, from Stone, Staffordshire, Donnelly's opponent in the
famous battle on the Curragh that lives on in song and in story.
Drawing by George Sharples.

From early morning on the day of the fight, 13 December 1815, every road leading to the Curragh was thronged, despite the rain that fell steadily until daybreak. No one had to ask the way, as they were all headed for the same place, Donnelly's Hollow. As for the fight with Tom Hall the previous year, it seemed as if every horse-drawn vehicle to be found was used to convey eager fans to the battle scene. Many others made their way on foot from Dublin and other distant locations. By ten o'clock, some 20,000 spectators occupied every available inch of Donnelly's Hollow and surrounding high-vantage points. A last-minute dispute over the purse money caused a delay and it looked like the fight might be called off. The original agreement was that the winner would receive £100 and the loser £20. Cooper was understandably angry when, on his arrival, he was told that not enough money had been raised to cover the initial terms. It would now be £60 for the victor and nothing for the man who lost. The Englishman refused to go through with the contest under these conditions and sat in his chaise for nearly an hour as the wrangle continued. Word of the dispute quickly spread through the crowd and there were fears of a riot if the fight was cancelled. Cooper eventually accepted that, in the interests of his health and safety, it would be wiser to go through with the contest.

" You'll Have to Fight!"

Cooper, told he would receive no payment if he lost, refuses to start the fight, but is persuaded to go ahead in fear of a riot. From Famous Fights, *date unknown.*

Polite applause greeted Cooper's appearance in the ring, while the thunderous cheers for the Irish champion's arrival could be heard in villages miles away. Ned Painter, who had seconded Hall in his clash with Donnelly, was back in Cooper's corner, while Dan was attended by Jack Coady. When the contestants 'came to scratch' in the centre of the ring, it was noticeable that, as against Hall, Donnelly had the physical advantages. Cooper, measuring five feet, ten inches and weighing twelve stone, was over two inches the shorter man and two stone the lighter. Considering their renowned hatred of training, both fighters looked surprisingly fit. Donnelly's condition was a tribute to the patience and perseverance of his trainer, Captain Barclay. It is an undeniable fact that had Dan continued to take such good care of his physical well-being, he would have enjoyed a longer boxing career – and extended his life. Alas, such concern was not part of his make-up.

After preliminary sparring, Donnelly landed the first punch, a heavy hook to the Englishman's neck. Cooper replied with a solid dig to the body. They went to close quarters, and 'desperate milling' ended with Donnelly, his greater strength already showing, knocking his rival to the ground. In his colourful account of the knockdown in *Boxiana*, Pierce Egan wrote: 'It would be impossible to describe the shout that accompanied this feat; it was not unlike the fire of artillery and the faces of the Paddies smiled again with innate approbation.'

In round two, both men displayed considerable defensive skill and it was some time before the first blow was struck, a 'sharp facer' from Donnelly. A follow-up punch made Cooper's ear bleed. 'First blood' to the local man and first bets settled. Donnelly drove his opponent to the ropes and again floored him. Cries of 'Bravo, Dan' and 'Ireland for ever' rang across the grassy plains of the Curragh. The English fighter was plainly upset at the crowd's partisanship, just as he was at the fury of their hero's aggression. Donnelly again dominated the third round and dealt out severe punishment. Cooper went down to another burst of wild cheering.

The visitor showed his great spirit by fighting back so strongly in the fourth round that the crowd was silenced. Cooper landed several solid thumps to Donnelly's head. When both men fell in a tangle to end the round, however, it was the Englishman who was underneath. The betting was now six to four on Donnelly. The fifth was a good round for Cooper. He pounded Dan about the head and then slipped neatly inside his guard to hurl him heavily onto his back with a mighty cross-buttock, a manoeuvre more akin to a wrestling tactic.

This was how *Fistiana* described it when advising young fighters:

> When your sides come together, you must manage to get your arm firmly over your adversary's neck, grasping his loose arm with the other hand – then shifting yourself to the front, get his crotch upon your hip or buttock, give him a cant over your shoulder. If well done, the heels will go up in the air, he goes over with tremendous violence and you fall upon his abdomen. The chances are

that he is either insensible or is so shaken by the fall that he loses all power of resisting your future attacks.

Captain Francis Grose, in *A Classical Dictionary of the Vulgar Tongue,* accurately summed up the cross-buttock as 'a particular lock or fall in the Broughtonian art which conveys more pleasurable sensations to the spectators than the patient'.

While Donnelly undoubtedly concurred with the latter sentiment, he seemed not too badly shaken by the throw and regained his feet without the aid of his seconds. The odds were now even. Cooper boxed brilliantly in the sixth round, his clever sidestepping of the Irishman's crude rushes even bringing applause from the home supporters. At last Dan got to grips with his slippery rival and managed to wrestle him to the turf, but not without difficulty. Feeling the fight might be going against him, he emerged from his corner for the seventh round with a look of grim determination. Aiming to show that his great strength would prove superior to the Englishman's scientific skill, he belted Cooper about the head with both fists. Then, in a colossal display of might, he tossed the smaller man to the ground with what was described as 'one of the most dreadful cross-buttocks ever witnessed'. For extra effect, he dropped on Cooper with all of his weight, 'driving the wind nearly out of his body'.

'The Bargeman' never recovered from the shock. He appeared much distressed on toeing the line for the eighth round and Donnelly wasted no time in following up his advantage. He hammered Cooper without respite and knocked him off his feet with a heavy left-hander. Amid the tumultuous applause, an Irish supporter could be heard offering 'a guinea to a tenpenny bit' on his man.

BANGING AND THUMPING HIM ALL OVER THE RING.

Donnelly staggers Cooper with a left-hander as his supporters shout encouragement and throw their hats in the air with delight.
From Famous Fights, *date unknown.*

Gallantly, Cooper fought back well in the ninth round and held his own in hard close-quarter exchanges. Donnelly, over-anxious to end the fight, missed with a ponderous swing and the momentum made him fall to the ground. By the tenth round, it was obvious that the Irish champion was simply too strong for his rival, now reduced to fighting on reserves of raw courage. Dan easily brushed aside his feeble efforts while countering with his own powerful blows. He threw Cooper down to climax the round.

Long odds were offered on Donnelly, but there were no takers. The brutal battle ended in the eleventh round. Cooper, showing magnificent spirit, made a brief rally and scored with some stinging hits. Donnelly, however, took all he had to offer and finished the proceedings with two terrific smashes to knock the Englishman senseless. The last punch broke Cooper's jaw. The fight had lasted twenty-two minutes.

Donnelly and Cooper in a close-quarter exchange while their seconds, inside the ring, watch intently.

As he strode up the hill towards his carriage, several of Donnelly's ecstatic supporters dug out the imprints of his feet. Known as 'the Steps to Strength and Fame', the markers are preserved in Donnelly's Hollow, leading from the monument commemorating his famous victory up to the rim of the hill. Visitors take delight in being able to walk, literally, in the footsteps of the conquering hero. They could hardly imagine the wild scenes that day nearly 200 years ago when Donnelly defeated Cooper.

Rich men offered the hospitality of their homes to the Irish champion. Peasants fought among themselves to get near to the hero and touch his brawny, sweaty back. Women waved silk handkerchiefs from the windows of their coaches in the hope they would be repaid with a smile. Dan did not disappoint them. Who could say if a simple gesture might not lead to more intimate contact when the immediate hubbub had died down?

Dan politely declined all the invitations to celebrate his triumph in the pubs of County Kildare. Mindful of how he had squandered the entire purse from his previous fight with Tom Hall, he said he had promised his family and friends he would return to Dublin immediately after the fight. If he thought he would get a more modest reception in the capital, he was mistaken. On his arrival in Townsend Street, his coach was besieged by admirers who informed Dan that the celebrations had already begun and begged him to join them in the Carlisle Tavern, opposite Carlisle Bridge (later reconstructed and re-named O'Connell Bridge). The festivities continued right through the night and Donnelly, after being called upon time after time to give his account of the Cooper fight, joined heartily in the singing and dancing to 'The Rakes of Kildare'.

The most remarkable aspect of the celebrations, according to an account in the *Dublin Penny Journal*, was the part played by the Irish champion's mother. In its issue of 25 August 1832, the newspaper looked back seventeen years to the eventful day:

> We remember well Donnelly's triumphal entry into Dublin after his great battle on the Curragh. That indeed was an ovation. He was borne on the shoulders of the people while his mother, like a Roman matron, leading the van in his procession and with all the pride of a second Agrippina, frequently slapped her naked bosom, exposed for the occasion, and exulting exclaimed: 'There's the breast that suckled him; there's the breast that suckled him.' Was the pride of a mother ever more admirably expressed?

Quite a woman was Donnelly's mother, by many accounts. An even more enchanting story about her was told to Antoine Raftery, the blind poet from County Mayo, by a former pugilist from Galway named O'Donnell. According to O'Donnell, Mrs Donnelly once won a 'fiver' in a six-mile race against a horse, which she won by several lengths. It seems that Dan was still an infant when his father one day met a member of a local foxhunt who boasted that he was the best horseman in the area. Joseph Donnelly retorted: 'Sure I know a woman, overburdened with a family, who could outpace you and your horse.' The incensed rider threatened he would have Donnelly run out of the country if he couldn't prove what he said, and demanded to know who this miracle woman was. 'Well, I left her at home behind me,' said Donnelly. 'She's my wife and if she runs three miles of the road going and coming, that's six miles, and you trotting, without galloping, and she going as fast as she can and she can't beat you, then you may do what you want with me.' The horseman said he would give him five pounds if his claim stood up. Joseph went home and told his wife of the challenge and the brave Mrs Donnelly, far from being put out, said: 'Oh, Joseph, it's a great supper we'll both be having tonight, seeing you wouldn't let him go full gallop.'

Dan's mother, leading the victory parade through the streets of Dublin, bares her bosom and proudly informs the crowd, 'There's the breast that suckled him.' From Famous Fights, *3 June 1901.*

The couple went to the horseman's home and the distance for the race was arranged and the place where they would turn around. Mrs Donnelly and the horse set off together and they were neck-and-neck at the turning point. At a quarter of a mile from the starting point, the woman turned to her rival and shouted; 'Are you not able to go any faster than that?' When she was 120 yards ahead, the rider ignored the agreement and put his horse into full gallop, but Mrs Donnelly finished first 'without being exhausted'. The horseman immediately handed Joseph the five pounds. 'The gentleman had a great respect for Donnelly and his wife ever afterwards,' said the storyteller. 'He said they came of good stock.'

One Irishman who did not share the general enthusiasm for Donnelly's win over Cooper was the hotel owner in Robertstown, County Kildare, who had been booked to prepare a victory banquet for the English pugilist and his friends. Cooper and his party had stayed at the hotel the night before the fight, having travelled from Dublin by canal barge. So confident were they of victory that a celebration dinner was ordered for forty guests. After his defeat, 'the Bargeman' and his company slipped quietly back to Dublin – this time by road – leaving an enraged hotelier with a kitchen-full of unwanted food and no payment.

As word spread across the Irish Sea of Donnelly's triumph, members of The Fancy were forced to revise their earlier contention that the Irishman was 'simply a big, clumsy rough'. *Boxiana* noted that Donnelly had 'shown improvement in both science and temper and was also in better condition than when he fought Hall. His superior strength enabled him to beat down the guard of Cooper with ease and effect.' *The Sporting Magazine* was even more enthusiastic: 'Since Donnelly fought Hall, we think there is no man could improve more than he has in fighting and if we may judge from his conduct this day, he has also improved in his temper. We venture to say that if he is to live regular and be advised by his friends, he would very soon be able to take the palm from the champion of England.'

Strength, determination, fitness and courage had all played a part in ensuring his victory. Legend informs us that there was another vital ingredient – a piece of confectionery! An enterprising Dublin character known as 'the Sugar Cane Man' did good business for several years through convincing members of the public that his magical product was responsible for saving Donnelly at a time in the fight when all seemed lost. The story was told by P.J. McCall, treasurer of the original Library Association of Ireland, in a paper entitled *In the Shadow of St Patrick's*, which he read before the National Literacy Society at their meeting on 27 April 1893. It was later published as a booklet.

'The Sugar Cane Man', as McCall remembered, came from Patrick Street, in the Liberties area of the city. A handsome little fellow dressed in a drab coat and white apron, he dispensed the sweets from a wooden tray suspended from a strap around his neck. In prose and verse, he would recite his product's wonderful benefits if taken regularly, and how it was responsible for 'the pleasant expression to be seen on every true Irishman's face'. He claimed that Donnelly was facing certain defeat against Cooper until Miss Kelly, Captain Kelly's sister, who had bet everything she possessed in the world on Dan winning, waved her hand in front of him and, with a bewitching smile, gave him a taste of the sugar cane while urging him: 'Now, me charmer, give him a warmer.' 'The result,' concluded the Sugar Cane Man, 'is a matter of history.'

Of the many street ballads written on the prize ring, the most popular and enduring was undoubtedly that commemorating Dan's defeat of Cooper. Up to the early part of the last century, when street ballads were still in vogue, Dan's great triumph would hold a crowd spellbound while the singer, for the few pennies his listeners could spare, bellowed out the seemingly never-ending verses.

Captain Kelly's sister pleads with Donnelly to rise from a knockdown and win as she had bet her entire estate on him beating Cooper. Pen-and-ink drawing by Jack B. Yeats, reproduced by courtesy of the Yeats Estate.

THE BALLAD OF DONNELLY AND COOPER

Come all you true-bred Irishmen, I hope you will
    draw near,
And likewise pay attention to these few lines I have
    here;
It is as true a story as ever you did hear
Of how Donnelly fought Cooper on the Curragh of
    Kildare.
It was on the third of June, brave boys, the challenge
    was sent o'er
From Britannia to old Grania for to raise her son
    once more
To renew the satisfaction and the credit to record,
They all in deep distraction since Daniel conquered all.
Old Grania read the challenge and received it with
    a smile,
'You'd better haste unto Kildare, my well beloved child,
It is there you'll reign victorious as you often did
    before
And your deeds will shine most glorious around sweet
    Erin's shore.'
When Donnelly and Cooper had stepped into the ring,
'Shake hands,' says Dan to Cooper, 'before we do
    begin,'
From nine to six they parried on, till Donnelly
    knocked him down;
Old Grania cried, 'Well done, my child, that's worth
    ten thousand pounds'.

The second round that Cooper fought he knocked
  down Donnelly,
But Dan had steel, likewise true pluck, and rose most
  manfully;
Right active then was Cooper and knocked Donnelly
  down once more;
The Englishmen, they all cried out, 'The battle is all
  our own.'
Long life unto Miss Kelly, 'tis recorded on the plain,
She boldly stepped into the ring saying 'Dan, what
  do you mean?'
Saying 'Dan, me boy, what do you mean? Hibernia's
  son,' says she,
'All my estate I have bet on you, brave Dan Donnelly.'
'Dan,' says she, 'that you're an Irishman the gentry
  all do know,
So on the Curragh of Kildare this day your valour
  show;
'Be sure you die before you fly, Hibernia's son,' says she,
'My coach and horses I have bet on you, Dan Donnelly.'
Donnelly rose up again and meeting with great might,
For to stagnate those nobles all, he continued with
  the fight;
Tho' Cooper stood in his own defence, exertion
  proved in vain,
For he soon received a temple blow that hurled him
  o'er the rails.
You sons of proud Britannia, your boasting now
  recall,

Since Cooper by Dan Donnelly has met his sad
   downfall;
In eleven rounds he got nine knockdowns, likewise a
   broke jawbone,
'Shake hand,' says she, 'brave Donnelly, the battle is
   all our own.'

'Donnelly and Cooper' provided the inspiration for many subsequent boxing ballads. Like the unknown composer of 'Donnelly and Cooper', the writers were very much concerned with the glorification of Ireland's struggle against British domination, as symbolized whenever an Irish fist bloodied an English nose. There are several instances. In 'The Glorious Victory of Paddy Murphy, our Irish Champion, over Johnny Batts, the English Bully, at Moyvalley', the composer, P.J. Fitzpatrick, tells of how Murphy draws new strength from remembering Donnelly's famous triumphs:

Remember Dan Donnelly in days that are gone by
He beat three English champions and their science
   did defy.
The Prince of Wales asked Donnelly, 'Are you old
   Ireland's boast?'
Said valiant Dan, 'I'm the best upon your English
   coast.'

After Batts, the Englishman, is beaten to the ground and 'lay there with many a wound and sore', the ballad writer gives him this parting advice:

Now Johnny Batts take my advice and quick as e'er
  you can,
To grope your way or get a guide and leave this
  Irish land,
And tell John Bull when you go home, in future
  to beware
To never fight an Irishman again in sweet Kildare.

In 'Heenan, the Bold Benicia Boy', the Irish-American
fighter John C. Heenan, whose father was from Clareen,
near Birr, in County Offaly, may have set the standard for
Muhammad Ali many years later when he boasted of his
forthcoming fight with the Englishman Tom Sayers:

I can lick him like a gander at any time I choose,
I can knock his very eyeballs from his forehead to
  his shoes,
Brave Donnelly was an Irishman who did for no
  man care,
Just as he walloped Cooper, I mean to beat Tom Sayers.

Unfortunately for Heenan, Sayers stoutly defied his best
efforts and the best he could achieve was a draw. Heenan
fell out of favour with the Irish when he was alleged to have
'sold' a fight against Tom King, an Englishman, in 1862.
He further blotted his copybook by refusing to support the
cause of Irish nationalism. The animosity Heenan engen-
dered is clear in the following extract from 'Coburn's Challenge to Heenan'. Joe Coburn, from Middletown, County
Armagh, makes clear his distaste for fighting a 'fellow Irishman' while demanding satisfaction by beating the 'traitor'.

Heenan, my boy, get ready and do not flinch from me
I'll show you the way that Cooper fell by Dan
　　Donnelly.
Money will not buy me, for gold I do not care,
I'll fight in defence of Paddy's Land and the laurel
　　that I wear.

Heenan must not have been too concerned as to what Coburn, or the rest of the Irish, thought of him, for he turned a deaf ear to Coburn's challenge. Coburn, who had a formidable reputation, then accused Jem Mace, the English champion, of running away from a proposed match. In 'The Cowardly Englishman', Dan Donnelly is once again upheld as the standard bearer of Irish heroism.

Our champion [Coburn] in great courage with his
　　seconds faced the ring,
But Mace, the cowardly bully, to his fight they could
　　not bring,
I'm sure he thought of Cooper when his jaw was
　　broke in two,
For Granua's sons were never beat in all that they
　　went through.

Yet another Irish pugilist whose blood was stirred by tales of the gallant exploits of Donnelly was John Morrissey, from Templemore, County Tipperary. Taken to America when he was three years old, Morrissey had a successful ring career before branching out into politics. He served two terms in the US Congress and was a State Senator for the Seventh District of New York. In 'The

Great Victory of John Morrissey over the Russian Sailor Boy' (depicting a fight in Tierra del Fuego, Argentina, for a $60,000-purse), the Irishman, five inches shorter and four stone lighter, beats his opponent so badly in thirty-eight rounds that doctors say he will never fight again. The penultimate verse of the ballad goes as follows:

> Our hero conquer'd Thompson and the Yankee
>   Clipper too,
> The Benicia Boy and Shepherd he so nobly did
>   subdue,
> Unto our bold Tipperary Boy the Russian forced to
>   yield,
> Brave Morrissey, like Donnelly, would die or gain
>   the field.

SIX

Publican and Playboy

Dan's purse of £60 for beating Cooper lasted for five weeks. He realized that prizefighting, with all its uncertainties, was no substitute for a steady job. His employer, however, told him bluntly that he would have to apply himself or look for alternative work. A short time later, a wealthy timber merchant (probably his boss at Connery's) made an attractive offer to the restless carpenter. He would set him up as a publican if he would promise to work hard and endeavour to make the business a success. Donnelly was delighted to accept.

Though Dublin was probably over-supplied with pubs, it was considered good business sense to install a popular sportsman as landlord. Pugilists, in particular, figured prominently on the lists of publicans in the major

British and Irish cities. Many of the leading English fight-ers, such as Tom Cribb, Tom Spring, Jack Randall, Ben Burns, 'Gentleman' John Jackson, Bill Richmond and Joe Ward, held the licences of premises in London. (Cribb's pub, the Union Arms in Panton Street, between Haymar-ket and Leicester Square, is still operating under the name 'The Tom Cribb'.) Bob Gregson ran the Castle Tavern in Holborn before moving to Ireland to take over a tavern in Moore Street, Dublin. Another former English champion, Tom Johnson, had the licence of his Dublin pub withdrawn 'from his house, not proving so consonant to the principles or propriety as were wished'. In other words, it was too rowdy. The consumption of alcohol was the most popular diversion for the Irish then, as it is now. In 1804, there were no fewer than fifty-five breweries and twenty-five distiller-ies located in the Dublin area alone. A census conducted half a century later showed that the Irish capital boasted the grand total of 2000 alehouses, 300 taverns and 1200 brandy shops. Many writers of the period condemned the excessive drinking of alcohol and called it a great national evil. The wretchedness of the social conditions was largely blamed for the population seeking to drown its sorrows in the consumption of alcohol.

The problem with installing 'celebrities' as landlords was that they were expected to mix freely with their cus-tomers. A sober publican might be able to avoid squander-ing much of his profits, but for someone as gregarious and fond of the bottle as Donnelly, it was a fatal occupation. As one contemporary writer explained, 'the landlord must drink with his friends or else be a churl … and should he again enter the ring he gives the chance away of two points out of three against himself'.

Nevertheless, Donnelly's premises in Poolbeg Street, close to where he grew up in Townsend Street, looked like proving a roaring success as customers flocked there to listen to the publican's stirring tales of the prize ring. On opening night, the timber merchant who owned the premises set up Donnelly with a supply of wine, spirits and porter to the value of £150. The Irish champion loved his new role and happily mingled with his customers and joined in their regular toasts to his health. Trade was so brisk in the first three months, it was said, that the barmen had no time for meal breaks. Dan felt like a man reborn. He married the girl he had been courting for some time and seemed ready and willing to accept his responsibilities as a husband and businessman. His mother was brought in to supervise the kitchen, while his wife helped to run the bar. As for boxing, Donnelly answered all enquiries with a firm declaration that he had no desire to re-enter the ring. Apart from taking part in occasional exhibition matches on benefit shows for pugilists who had fallen on hard times, he devoted all of his energy to running the pub.

The probability that Donnelly had retired from the ring brought consternation to his faithful followers. In England, too, members of The Fancy were disappointed that they would not see for themselves if he deserved his fine reputation. George Cooper had, on his return home after his defeat in Donnelly's Hollow, suggested that there was no one to equal his conqueror among the top English pugilists. It had been strongly rumoured that Cooper, as a result of his savage beating, was disabled and confined to his room in London. *The Sporting Magazine* even reported Cooper's 'death' a few weeks after the fight. Though unfounded, the reports served to add to Donnelly's standing as 'a formidable buffer'. Pierce Egan, whose evaluation of prizefighters was considered second to none, gave a glowing assessment of Donnelly's attributes in *Boxiana*:

> He is in possession of every requisite to constitute a first-rate boxer. He is in height about six feet, weighing fourteen stone, gifted with prodigious strength, no lack of courage, a good knowledge of the science and backed with the prime advantages of youth, being under thirty years of age. The blows of Donnelly are described as terrific and appalling and in their operation more like the ponderosity of a sledgehammer than given from the arm of a human being, added to which he has a peculiar sort of hitch, or fastening, that gives him great facility in cross-buttocking his opponents when in the act of closing. He has an animated countenance and his head altogether portrays a staunch milling index.

Dan spurned every effort to entice him back into the ring. Circumstances, however, brought about a change of mind. The initial excitement of life as a publican began to pall and he fell back into his irresponsible ways. Business and family welfare took second place to heavy drinking sessions with his cronies. Often he would not appear at the pub for days, leaving the running of the business to his over-burdened wife. Unscrupulous customers took advantage of the landlord's absence to slip away without paying. Mrs Donnelly was either too busy to notice or physically incapable of stopping them. When Dan sobered up for long enough to be told he was tossing away a lucrative living, he appeared to take heed and promised to settle down. It didn't last long and trade fell away when the main attraction failed to appear. Donnelly finally came to his senses, but too late to save the business. He had run up heavy debts through his neglect and his expensive drinking binges. There seemed to be only one way of his troubles – by making a return to the ring.

He went back into light training while efforts were made to find one of the leading English pugilists willing to travel to Ireland to fight him. There was no rush of volunteers. If his formidable reputation did not scare them off, it was feared they would not get a fair deal tackling an Irishman on his own soil. Tom Hall had claimed he was cheated of victory when Donnelly punched him while he was on the ground. George Cooper said that, along with not getting paid, he found that the Irish fans were prepared to go to any lengths to ensure that their man won. One of his seconds, Ned Painter, complained that he had been struck by a stone thrown into the ring. It was clear that if Donnelly wanted a fight, he would have to go to England. This he was not prepared to do.

He decided to have another go at running a pub, this time securing the licence of premises in the historic Liberties area of Dublin. The Capstan Bar, at the corner of the Coombe and New Row, is still trading under the name of John Fallon and Sons. During his spell there, Donnelly lived across the road, at the corner of Francis Street. He felt he had made a mistake taking the previous pub in Poolbeg Street as it was too close to Townsend Street, where he was born and grew up, and he was expected to dole out complimentary drinks to the many people he knew. The Coombe seemed to be suitably distant from the freeloaders, but Dan soon discovered that his fan club extended to the Liberties, with the same disastrous consequences. He fell back into his old reckless ways and proved he was a flop as a businessman. Whatever profits he made were frittered away and his debts piled up. It was the same sad story when he took over his third pub, at 89 Capel Street.

After a heart-to-heart talk with his family and close friends, Donnelly agreed that there was only one course open to him. He would have to go to England and try to cash in on his boxing reputation. His aim was not to engage in prizefights, just in exhibition matches. Decent money could be earned by 'showing off' and he should make enough to be able to pay off his debts. He got in touch with Jack Carter, reckoned by many to be the best fighter in England, whom he had first met when Carter seconded Tom Hall against him. Carter readily accepted the Irishman's offer to engage in a series of exhibition bouts. The news of Donnelly's arrival in England aroused much interest among The Fancy. Now they would get the chance to see for themselves what the much-hyped Irishman was made of.

Dan bid a reluctant farewell to his family and set sail on the packet steamer from Ringsend to Liverpool. The monotony of the eighteen hours at sea was relieved by 'a few glasses of whiskey and a sound forty winks'. By prior arrangement, he was met on arrival by an Irish innkeeper named Regan, who offered him free lodgings for as long as he wanted to stay in Liverpool. The hospitality lavished upon the Irish champion by the Liverpool Irish was hardly conducive to his getting into proper physical shape for the proposed boxing programme. His landlord threw regular all-night parties and Dan joined in with gusto. He revelled in his new-found freedom and lost no time in proving his charm with the opposite sex, although he would invariably voice his regrets for giving in to 'the temptations of the flesh', blaming it on 'the demon drink'. While alcohol was known to make some boxers aggressive, in Donnelly's case it made him amorous.

An unsavoury incident on the night before he left Liverpool for Manchester, where he had arranged to meet Carter, typified his shameless behaviour. Regan put on a farewell party and it was well after midnight when Donnelly slumped across a table. His senses were not so dulled that he failed to notice a pretty young maid smiling in his direction. He thought it strange that he had not noticed her up to then, as Regan's servants were familiar to him. The girl approached him.

'Mr Donnelly,' she said, 'you do look tired. Let me take you to your room.' Dan mumbled his gratitude and placed his arm around the girl's slim shoulders as she helped him climb the two flights of stairs. On reaching his room, she led him inside and locked the door behind them. The next morning, the landlord's throbbing head was in no way relieved by the thumping of a heavy fist on his bedroom door, accompanied by the enraged shouts of his special guest. 'What's the matter, Dan?' groaned Regan. 'My money and my clothes, they're gone,' exclaimed Donnelly. 'I have to meet Carter in Manchester in a few hours and all I can find are my shirt and pants.'

Regan was puzzled. The two men searched the house from top to bottom, but there was no sign of the missing items. It was only when Donnelly explained about the girl taking him to his room that the truth dawned on Regan. He did not have a maid answering Dan's description. Obviously, the girl was an unscrupulous type who had slipped into the tavern when everyone was too drunk to notice her and, posing as a maid, had chosen her all-too-willing victim. Cursing his stupidity, Donnelly was concerned with how he would carry out his rendezvous with Carter. Regan proved himself a true friend by getting a local tailor to fit the much-relieved Irishman with a suit and provided him with enough money to tide him over his initial stay in Manchester.

SEVEN

Facing the Sceptical English

The following notice was posted at various locations in Manchester and in the local press:

> Donnelly, Champion of Ireland, and Carter, Champion of England, will exhibit together in various combats the art of self-defence at the Emporium Rooms on February 18, 1819.

While Donnelly's claim to recognition as Irish champion was valid, Carter was taking a bit of a liberty in announcing himself as the English titleholder. That honour still belonged to Tom Cribb, even though he had not fought for eight years. Carter, billed as 'the Lancashire Hero', was a talented, scientific boxer with a punishing left hand – he used his right sparingly – and was undoubtedly one of his country's leading boxers, though it was noted that he lacked staying power. His record showed wins over George Cooper and Tom Oliver, but he did not distinguish himself in an encounter with Tom Molineaux when, with victory within his grasp, he suddenly caved in. A canal navigator by occupation, Carter was credited with many talents besides boxing. He won twelve out of fourteen racing and walking races. A good dancer, he 'performed the clog hornpipe with considerable ability', and was renowned for being able to drink several pints of ale while standing on his head! Sadly, his successful partnership with Donnelly would end in a bitter, prolonged row that reflected little credit on Carter, even among his fellow countrymen.

Whether the Manchester boxing fans accepted Carter's claim to the championship of England or not, the first exhibition match with Donnelly attracted a sell-out crowd to the Emporium Rooms. When the pair moved on to Liverpool and other locations, similar 'full house' signs went up. The Fancy, anxious to see if the Irish champion lived up to the reputation that had preceded him across the Irish Sea, were not disappointed. Indeed, it was widely believed that the Irish might have found a fighting man capable of matching the best in England and beyond. Pierce Egan gave his assessment in *Boxiana*: 'The Irish champion is an acknowledged first-rate boxer and from the repeated use of the gloves, he has derived great improvement. The size, strength and science of Donnelly qualify him to fight any man in the world.'

The sceptical Londoners, however, reserved their judgments until they saw him perform. Growing demand for

Dan to appear in the metropolis forced him to overcome his initial reticence. He was well aware of the temptations the big city would offer and how easily he could be drawn in. Still, London was the place to go if real money was to be made, so that's where Donnelly and Carter headed.

The excited chatter of Irish migrants competed with the calmer discussions among the English as Donnelly made his London debut at the Peacock Theatre, in Gray's Inn Road, on 18 March. The audience was well pleased with the fare on offer. It was generally felt that Donnelly's strength and powerful punching was balanced by the more scientific style and superior mobility of Carter. *Boxiana* again provided the authoritative voice:

> The difference in styles was most marked. Carter, an agile, confident dancing master, walking round and round, picking his blows with the perfection of a professor. Donnelly is not so showy, but he is dangerous. He is no tapper [light puncher], nor does he throw his blows away. He makes tremendous use of the right hand. Nor is he to be got at without encountering mischief. He is, however, awkward. His attitude [stance] was not admired and it was thought he leaned too far back, inclining to his right shoulder. But final judgement cannot be pronounced from sparring, more especially as Donnelly does not profess use of the gloves. It was a close affair with honours about even.

The following Thursday, Donnelly topped the bill at the Minor Theatre, in Catherine Street, off The Strand. A new sparmate, Ben Burns, a boxer of considerable class, exposed the Irishman's scientific limitations. Dan's habit of standing too far back and leaning away made it difficult for him to counter-punch effectively, but his constant aggression and attempts to land his hard punches made the match interesting. The set-to was loudly applauded. Donnelly finished the night's proceedings by boxing a few sharp rounds with Carter. Supporters of the Irishman, while ready to concede that he did not impress too well in gloved sparring sessions, boasted that, in a proper bare-knuckle battle to the finish, no prizefighter in England could match him.

The call went out for Donnelly to take the supreme test – a clash with Tom Cribb, the undisputed champion of England. That the contest never took place is a great pity. The Irishman's detractors always felt that, because he never fought top-ranked contemporaries like Cribb and Tom Spring, his true worth was much exaggerated by his starry-eyed countrymen. While this view is hard to dispute, there is no denying that Dan's renowned strength and punching power, together with his courage and unquenchable will to win, would have made him a decent bet against any fighter of his era. Had the match with Cribb come off, it is not fanciful to suggest that Donnelly would have emerged the winner of a long, exhausting encounter. His endurance and refusal to yield might have forced the English champion to concede defeat. After all, Cribb was then aged thirty-eight and had not fought since his gruelling return match with Tom Molineaux eight years earlier. As for Tom Spring, Cribb's successor as English champion, he was a much better stylist than Donnelly, but was not nearly as heavy a hitter. Spring suffered from brittle hands that caused him to pick up some unflattering nicknames, such as 'the Lady's Maid' and 'the Powder-puff Fighter'. His weakness might have proved costly in a prolonged set-to with the Irishman.

The growing demand for a showdown between the champions of England and Ireland seemed to be successful when it was announced that Cribb and Donnelly would box at the Minor Theatre in a charity tournament for Bob Gregson. It would, of course, be merely an exhibition with the contestants wearing gloves, but it would provide some indication as to how the rivals might shape up in a real fight. The date, 1 April, proved significant. It was an April Fool hoax. Donnelly turned up as scheduled, but there was no sign of Cribb. The mood of the packed house grew even angrier when it was announced that Donnelly could not box as he had injured his arm falling off the Oxford stagecoach. Fearing a riot, the promoters pleaded with Dan to put on the gloves and spar a few rounds with Jack Carter. Donnelly agreed and the crowd was pacified, but not for long. It was quickly apparent that Dan was unable to block punches with his badly bruised and swollen right arm and the bout would have to be cut short. Carter did not wish to add to his sparmate's discomfort and, as a result, few blows were attempted by either man before the affair was terminated. Loud booing followed the contestants as they left the stage.

A member of the audience, Harry Sutton, one of several American black boxers who had sought to progress his career in England, was so encouraged by Donnelly's tame showing that he climbed onto the stage to publicly challenge him to a bare-knuckle fight for £50-a-side. The crowd, now clearly against Donnelly, called on him to accept the challenge. Bill Richmond, acting on the Irishman's behalf, entered the ring to state that Donnelly 'did not come to England with any intention of entering the prize-ring'. This was greeted by another storm of booing and abuse directed at Donnelly.

Dan could be seen whispering to Carter and the latter then announced that Donnelly would consult with his friends in Ireland and England about the possibility of fighting Sutton. The American, to loud cheers, said he would be willing to fight Donnelly at five minutes' notice for £50, or for £100 or £200 at any agreed time. Dan, upset at the insinuations of cowardice, had the following notice printed in the London newspapers a few days later:

> At a sparring match for the benefit of Gregson, on Thursday the first day of April, Donnelly, having met with an accident, hopes the public will pardon him if he has not amused the gentlemen present to their satisfaction. After the set-to between Harmer and Sutton, the latter thought proper to come forward and challenge any man, and Donnelly in particular, for £50, £100 or £200. Donnelly, being something of a stranger, did not come forward to answer the challenge until he should first consult his friends in this country and in Ireland, but he has confidence that his friends will back him. He therefore begs leave to say that he did not come to England for the purpose of fighting, but it appears to

be the wish of the gentlemen here to try his mettle. He begs leave further to say that he will fight any man in England of his weight for £100 to £500.

No more was heard of the proposed Sutton fight and Donnelly, while awaiting replies to his open challenge, continued with his series of exhibitions. His standing with The Fancy had taken a considerable plunge, however, and it did not help his cause when another publicized sparring match with Cribb, at the Fives Court, in Little Saint Martin's Street, failed to come off.

Tom Cribb, celebrated champion of England from 1809 to 1822, was billed to meet Donnelly in several exhibition matches that failed to take place. From a mezzotint by Charles Turner after an oil painting by Douglas Guest.

As Donnelly and Carter entered the ring that evening, they were met by a chant of 'Cribb, Cribb, Cribb'. The upset Irish champion threatened to withdraw from the exhibition, but it was Carter, even angrier at the poor reception, who stormed off the stage. The audience became more subdued when they realized they might get no show for their money, and they called for Carter to return, only to find that 'the Lancashire Hero' had left the building. Harry Harmer took his place against Donnelly. Plainly unhappy and still suffering discomfort from his injured arm, Dan boxed well below form and Harmer had much the better of the exchanges. The Irishman wore a pained expression as he left the ring to more hissing and booing. Pierce Egan, in *Boxiana*, criticized the crowd's behaviour: 'It was very unlike the usual generosity of John Bull towards a stranger. It was not national, but savoured of something like prejudice. Such partialities ought not to be exhibited.'

There was only one way Donnelly could win the respect of the English – by beating one of their top men in a fight to the finish. It was to the delight of all that he announced he had accepted a challenge from Tom Oliver for a match at 100 guineas-a-side. Oliver's challenge had been made during a benefit show for Sam Martin at the Fives Court. Donnelly was not present, but Jack Randall accepted on his behalf.

Dan, determined to show the sceptical English he was every bit as good as his countrymen claimed, gave his more impressive display to date in an exhibition with Carter at the Minor Theatre on 27 April. He cleverly blocked most

Standing room only was the order of the day at the Fives Court in London when leading prizefighters, such as Donnelly, sparred with gloves. The boxers in this illustration are Jack Randall and Ned Turner. From an aquatint by Charles Turner after T. Blake.

of the Englishman's best punches and took the grin off Carter's face with some stinging right-handers. Carter was preparing to fight Tom Spring a week later and might have been more intent on avoiding injury than fully exerting himself. Nevertheless, there was much praise for Donnelly's improved showing. Dan was saddened to see his friend going down to defeat against Spring after one hour and fifty-five minutes of hard battling, and afterwards asked the winner if he would consent to meeting him in an exhibition. Spring was glad to oblige and the bout was scheduled for the Minor Theatre on 25 May.

Tom Spring, successor to Tom Cribb as English champion, boxed an exhibition with Donnelly at the Minor Theatre in London in May 1819. From a coloured print by W.E. Dowling after a painting by J. Jackson.

Donnelly, awaiting final arrangements for the fight with Oliver, was at the peak of his form against Spring. He blocked many of Tom's best blows with admirable skill and his alertness in skipping away and returning to the attack drew loud applause. Though it was only an exhibition, it was a performance of considerable merit by the Irishman. Spring, whose real name was Winter, was rated one of the most skilled of the bare-knuckle bruisers, and later scribes would describe him as 'the James J Corbett of his time'. He was only beaten once – by Ned Painter – in his ten-year career, and captured the championship of England on Tom Cribb's exit. Spring retired in 1824 after twice beating Irishman Jack Langan in lengthy duels. Donnelly's ability to shine in his encounter with Spring led to the observation that he had either acquired considerable skill since arriving in England or he had been hiding his true talents.

Final details of the fight with Tom Oliver were worked out when the boxers and their backers gathered at Dignam's tavern, the Red Lion, in Haughton Street, Clare Market. One of Donnelly's patrons was a well known general in sporting circles who, shortly after Dan stepped foot on British soil, personally tested the visitor's ability. After being sent reeling by a fierce blow to the face, the general was convinced that Donnelly was worthy of his support.

EIGHT

Training – It's a Bore!

Wheeler's, a popular training camp for pugilists at Riddlesdown, three miles from Croydon in Surrey, was chosen for Donnelly's preparation for the Oliver fight. Modern boxers, who can spend many weeks of strenuous work preparing for a fight, often express amazement, and some amusement, at the comparatively simple training routines of the bare-knuckle breed. Great emphasis was placed upon long walks and some sprinting to build up stamina for long, exhausting contests. Apart from sparring practice, light exercise and 'the avoidance of excesses, either in food, wine or women', little more was considered necessary. *Fistiana* gave the following advice to pugilists:

> Each day, rise with the sun. Wash. Trot (the extreme pace of toe and heel) for one mile to three. Eat a dry

biscuit. Run home. Have breakfast, lasting ten to fifteen minutes and consisting of boiled mutton or beef
and potatoes. Rub down, lasting half an hour, and then
walk until about eleven o'clock, during which one to
three miles should be run at top speed. A rest to talk
to patron and, at twelve noon, a sparring bout lasting
about an hour and imitating in earnestness and length
the prospective fight. About two o'clock have dinner,
lasting not more than an hour and consisting of the
same diet. Then more walking exercise and to bed with
the sun.

It was Captain Barclay, Donnelly's trainer, who first
drew the attention of the boxing world to the inestima-
ble benefits of correct preparation. His most acclaimed
feat was in reducing the weight of Tom Cribb, who 'from
his mode of living in London and the confinement of a
crowded city, had become corpulent, big-bellied, full of
gross humours and short-breathed', from sixteen stone
to thirteen stone, five pounds in nine weeks. Barclay was
a great believer in regular movement of the bowels and
prescribed regular doses of physic. As for food and drink,
he insisted that 'veal and lamb should never given, not
vegetables such as turnips, carrots or potatoes, as they are
watery and difficult to digest. Neither butter or cheese is
allowed. Eggs are also forbidden, except the yolk taken raw
in the morning. Liquors must always be taken cold and
home-brewed beer, old but not bottled, is the best. Water
must never be given and ardent spirits are strictly prohib-
ited, how ever diluted.' Barclay was adamant on one other

point: 'The sexual intercourse must vanish and be no more heard of within the first week of training.'

While Cribb obviously thrived on Barclay's strict regimen, as did the captain himself, there is little doubt that Donnelly found it all too regimental to his way of thinking. He was so convinced that excess of any kind would not hurt him that he acted as he pleased. Dan's own opinion of how a boxer should prepare for a bout is something of a classic in its own right. Asked for advice by fellow Dubliner Jack Langan, who had an important contest coming up the next day, Donnelly said:

> First, take off your shirt. Then walk up and down the room briskly and hit out well with both hands. Jump backwards and forwards at least 100 times. As it is now midnight, go home directly, drink half a gallon of the sourest buttermilk you can find and go to bed. At five o'clock in the morning, not a minute later, you must get up and run three or four miles. And at every mile you must swig – not whiskey, mind you – but a quart of spring water.

Langan, following his idol's instructions as faithfully as he could, had only a few hours' sleep before rising at dawn. After knocking up all the dairymen in the neighbourhood, all he could get was three pints of buttermilk. To make up the deficiency, he drank a larger quantity of water. Considering the extremes he had gone to, it is not surprising that he arrived half an hour late for the fight. His opponent was just leaving the ring when he arrived, full of apologies.

Langan struggled through the early rounds before eventually gaining the upper hand and winning after thirty-five minutes. It is a matter of conjecture whether Donnelly's tuition had aided his ability to win or had prevented him from scoring a quicker victory.

Jack Langan, Dan's successor as champion of Ireland, saw his relationship with his idol soured in a dispute over the ending of Langan's fight with Pat Halton, who was seconded by Donnelly. From a drawing by W.L. Thomas.

But then Donnelly was hardly the best man from whom to seek advice on training. To him, the task of getting down to even a half-strict routine was a bore. He longed for the day of the fight when it would be over and done with. It was normal for a pugilist to have a close companion to see that he observed the programme set out for him, but Donnelly made sure that no one put reins on him. His most constant companion at Riddlesdown, according to one observer, was a bottle of whiskey. He even took it to bed with him. He claimed he needed 'a small drop of stuff to make me sleep'.

'At other times,' disclosed *Boxiana*, 'he stole out in the dark like a poacher to procure "game" – and the preserves of Croydon supplied more than his needs.'

It was obvious that the 'game' he bagged was not of the feathered variety. He took nobody's advice but his own, and would make a joke of anyone's suggestions that his training methods were, to say the least, unorthodox. On one occasion at Riddlesdown, a fellow diner who noticed him helping himself to large quantities of green peas suggested that peas were hard to digest and therefore unsuitable for a boxer in training.

'Sure a few peas won't harm me,' laughed the Irish champion, 'no more than a drop of the cratur. And now I'll show you how I'll take the peas and the liquor out of me.' With that, he left the dining room and ran up a steep hill in front of Wheeler's house, returning a few minutes later in a state of perspiration, still grinning broadly. All things considered, he looked in remarkably good condition on the day of the fight. Pierce Egan published his observations in *Boxiana*: 'On stripping, Donnelly exhibited as fine a picture of a human frame as can be imagined. His legs were firm and well-rounded, his arms slingy and powerful. The tout ensemble indicated prodigious strength.'

Tom Oliver, who had trained diligently for the fight, was said to be in the best condition of his career. 'His flesh was as firm as a rock,' noted Egan. In Donnelly's case, his appearance was deceptive. Both during the fight and afterwards, it was clear that his reckless lifestyle was taking its toll.

One of the Englishman's backers called upon Donnelly the day before the fight and attempted to undermine his confidence by predicting: 'About this time tomorrow you can expect a pretty head from the fists of Oliver.' Dan looked him straight in the eye and replied: 'I was not born in a wood to be frightened by an owl.' The nobleman offered to bet £10 to £15 on his countryman, which Donnelly gladly accepted.

NINE

The Battle with Tom Oliver

The rain fell in torrents on the morning of 21 July 1819. To compound the misery of those who had arrived early at Bledlow Common, Buckinghamshire, to gain good viewing positions, they were informed that the venue had been switched to Crawley Downs in Sussex, sixty-two miles away. The reason the organizers made the last-minute change was for fear of the law intervening. Prizefighting was illegal, not because of its brutality, as might be imagined, but for fear of crowd disturbances. So many fights were 'fixed' that it was labelled a crooked sport and minor riots sometimes broke out when a boxer clearly 'sold out' and those who bet on him refused to pay out. In spite of the ban, which lasted until 1901, prizefights were staged regularly, usually in places where the local magistrates and police were sympathetic and turned a blind eye.

The realization that the Donnelly–Oliver encounter would not be held in Bledlow was a particularly sad blow to the youngsters who had been up at the crack of dawn, made their way in the pouring rain, and climbed trees to secure their 'roosting places' overlooking the site. Only the hardiest was prepared to face the long extra journey to Crawley Downs. It was a disappointment, too, for Oliver, as Bledlow was his home patch. He was born there in 1789.

The contest generated great interest among The Fancy, both in Britain and Ireland. Many of Donnelly's supporters made the journey across the Irish Sea to witness their hero's first fight on English soil. They were confident he would prove that the boasts about his ability were not exaggerated. Many Englishmen shared that view. By the time of the fight, Dan was the seven-to-one favourite. Betting was not just on the result, but on who would gain 'first blood', or if the odds switched in Oliver's favour at any stage during the fight.

In an age of wide class divisions, boxing attendance was a great social leveller. 'Gentlemen' did not raise too many objections when required to mix with the lower orders in order to enjoy the thrill of the event. 'Around a prize ring,' observed Pierce Egan, 'every greasy hero or sooty chief placed himself by the side of the swells without any apology as feeling he had the right to do so. Selection is entirely out of the question … the noble lord and the needy commoner are both at home after they have paid their tip for admission.'

The Fancy, over their beer and 'baccy', enjoying a sparring match between two unidentified pugilists. Adorning the walls are sketches of famous boxers of the day. From a drawing believed to be by George Cruikshank.

The Fancy was generally understood to include all those who followed or were involved in pugilism, the fighters, the patrons, the trainers, the audiences, all those whose 'fancy' was the prize ring. Egan and many of his contemporaries insisted that the term was not restricted to followers of boxing, but embraced other 'fancied' sports such as cock-fighting, dog-fighting, and bear- and badger-baiting. William Hazlitt accused The Fancy of having no imagination, of restricting their topics of conversation to fighting men and dogs, and to bears and badgers. Another writer deplored the fact that they scarcely ever opened their mouths without the finishing line, 'I'll bet you two-to-one or six-to-four.'

Sometimes a fair-minded 'toff' would strike a blow for the rights of the commoner. The Duke of Clarence, later King William IV, was in attendance at a fight at Moulsey Hurst when he heard a nobleman expressing his distaste at the rough-looking element of the crowd. The duke delivered the put-down remark: 'Be pleased to recollect, my lord, that we are all Englishmen here.'

Pierce Egan's *Life in London* relates the surprise felt by the provincial, Jerry, when he visits the Royal Cockpit in Tufton Street, London, and finds 'flue-fakers [chimney sweeps] dustmen, lamp-lighters, stagecoachmen, bakers, farmers, barristers, swells, butchers, dog-fanciers, grooms, donkey-boys, weavers, snobs, market-men, watermen, honourables, sprigs of the nobility, MPs, mailguards, swaddies, etc., all in rude contact, jostling and pushing against each other when the doors were opened to procure a front seat'.

Tom, the Corinthian, explains to his country cousin, Jerry: 'They are all sporting characters and are all touched more or less with the scene before them; and the flue-faker will drop his bender [sixpence] with as much pluck as the honourable does his fifty to support his opinion. The spirit is the same and it is only the blunt [money] that makes the difference.'

Oliver was the first of the contestants to arrive at the fight scene in Crawley Downs, at 1.30 pm. He tossed his hat into the ring to signify that he was ready to do battle. He was seconded by Tom Cribb and Tom Shelton, while the noble lord who was his patron was in close attendance. Donnelly made his way to the ring to loud cheers from his fellow countrymen. 'Success to you, Dan,' they shouted, and 'Ireland for ever.'

The fighters stripped and tied their coloured silk hand-kerchiefs to one of the wooden stakes that held up the ropes. The green silk of Ireland was placed over the blue for England. It was customary for the winner to take both silks. Oliver's striped silk stockings drew much comment and amusement. Donnelly was attended by Tom Belcher and Jack Randall. In the bare-knuckle era, the seconds stayed inside the ring during the contest. One, 'the bottle man', administered refreshment to his fighter between rounds, while the other was 'the knee man', who would go down on one knee and allow his other knee to be used as a seat by the boxer. Apparently, no one thought of bringing a stool!

Donnelly's opponent was more renowned for his out-standing courage than his boxing skill or punching power, but he was more experienced than the Irishman, number-ing among his victims Ned Painter, Ned Hopping, Harry Lancaster, William Ford and Black Kendrick. He had beaten Donnelly's last opponent, George Cooper, in sev-enteen minutes, quicker than Dan had managed. It was in his losing battles with Jack Carter and Bill Neat that Oliver earned respect as 'bravest of the brave'. Described by one writer as 'a thick-eared old warrior with a mug like a map of the United Kingdom', Oliver finished his ring career by taking a fierce beating from Tom Spring in a contest lasting fifty-five minutes. He was nicknamed 'the Battersea Gardener' after his place and job of work. Apart from his ring success, he was respected for his successes in walking, running and trotting races, and for his ability to organize 'scientific dog fights' and bull-baiting.

Tom Oliver, from Bledlow, in Buckinghamshire, bravely stood up to Donnelly for thirty-four rounds at Crawley Downs, Sussex, in July 1819. From a drawing by George Sharples.

Donnelly and Oliver toed the line at 2 pm, much later than scheduled because of the hitch in fixing the site. Both men looked calm and confident. No blows were struck for the first minute as the combatants warily sized each other up. The Irish champion attempted the first punch, a left that fell short of its target. Again he tried and again he was out of range. Angered at his futile efforts, Dan stepped up his attack and drove the Englishman back against the ropes. They grappled as each tried desperately to throw the other man to the ground. After much exertion, they went down together, with Donnelly on top. The round had lasted five minutes.

Oliver tried a heavy blow in the second round, but Donnelly cleverly blocked it with his forearm. There was another tussle by the ropes before they fell, the Irishman again uppermost. When he returned to 'the scratch' for the next round, Oliver was bleeding from the nose and was already showing signs of distress. It was 'first blood' then to Donnelly. The Englishman attacked bravely and forced Dan to retreat to the ropes, where both tumbled to the turf, amid cries of 'Well done, Oliver.'

Feeling encouraged, Oliver tried a body attack, but was unable to get through his opponent's tight guard. Tom did connect with one heavy right to the ribs, but had to take a vicious left to the face, which staggered him backwards. At close quarters, Donnelly was 'tied up', so he butted Oliver in the face, an unsporting tactic that drew loud protests from the Englishman's supporters. Dan employed his great strength to throw his rival to the ground with considerable force. Oliver looked badly shaken when he rose.

It was Donnelly's turn to shed blood in the fifth round after taking a heavy smash to the mouth, preceded by a solid dig to the stomach that brought down his guard. Once again, however, Dan's strength told at close range when he threw his rival down with a cross-buttock. Cautious sparring marked the start of round six. Light blows were exchanged for about five minutes until Donnelly dropped 'the Battersea Gardener' with a solid right under the heart. Unable to check his attack in time, Dan appeared to strike his opponent when he was down. The Englishman's corner yelled 'Foul' but after consultation between the umpires representing each boxer, it was ruled to be accidental. The blood flowed freely in the seventh round – Oliver from the nose and Donnelly from the mouth – following some lively exchanges. Oliver got through with a good barrage to the body and nipped away smartly from Dan's attempted counters. The Irish champion was floored to end the round, the best to date for Oliver, who grinned broadly as he rested on his second's knee.

Donnelly appeared unruffled after the thirty seconds' break. After slipping to the turf, he nearly caused Oliver to fall over him. The Englishman's seconds accused Dan of 'lifting his leg with intent to kick Oliver or divert him from his purpose'. This was hotly denied by the Irish side and the fight was allowed to continue. The pair wrestled and then fell together. Oliver was bleeding profusely. In the ninth, Donnelly pulled away from a clinch and hit out strongly, although it was noticeable that he was relying mainly on his left hand. He did use his right to land a solid dig to Tom's ribs and knock him down. Such was the impact of the punch that the mark of the Irishman's fist was evident for the rest of the fight.

Both boxers and their seconds were alert for any opportunity to gain an advantage, fairly or otherwise. When

Oliver was knocked down in the tenth round, his corner-man, Shelton, stuck out his knee to cushion the fall. Tom Belcher, Donnelly's attendant, was so incensed that he shouted a warning to Shelton not to try it again. Shelton insisted that his knee just happened to be in that position as Oliver fell.

There was much discussion among the crowd about Donnelly's sparing use of his right hand, about which the Irish had bragged so much. Was the 'sledgehammer right' just a fanciful Irish yarn? The eleventh and twelfth rounds were tamely contested, with Donnelly each time finishing uppermost in the falls. Twenty-four minutes had now elapsed and it was the Englishman who looked the more tired. Right from 'scratch' in the thirteenth, Dan hit his opponent flush in the mouth and stunned him. Gamely, Oliver rallied and the pair wrestled in the middle of the ring, trying to gain a throw. Donnelly pulled clear and landed a heavy blow to the throat that left the Englishman hanging helplessly on the ropes. Dan sportingly stood back and lifted his arms, refusing to take advantage. Oliver, too exhausted to be grateful, slumped slowly to the turf.

The English fans had not had much to cheer about up to now, but they enjoyed a brief moment of elation in the fourteenth round when their man staggered Donnelly with 'a hard facer'. Their enthusiasm was quickly stifled when the Irishman stormed back to beat Tom to the ground. In the fifteenth session, Oliver reeled before Donnelly's attack and went down beside the ropes. Both men showed the effects of their gruelling ordeal in the next when they fell together and their respective seconds had to prise the tangled bodies apart. After some heavy exchanges in the seventeenth round, Donnelly mounted a firm offensive and Oliver was forced to beat a hasty retreat. Looking very disheartened and bleeding badly, he slumped to the ground. Dan fell on top of him and his knee caught Oliver in the stomach. Cries of 'Foul' from the English corner were dismissed by the umpires. Both men dropped together to end an uneventful eighteenth round. A gallant rally by Oliver in the next round petered out and he fell flat on his face.

Round twenty: one of Donnelly's rare rights caught his rival on the eye, but there was little force behind it and Oliver just grinned. Dan connected with two good lefts to the head before a wrestling session ended with both men on the ground, this time with the Irishman underneath. 'Well done, Oliver' was the chant from the English fans. The next three rounds were scrappy, with few clean blows landed and each session ending with the boxers falling together as they wrestled. The spectators, who had not been treated to their anticipated satisfaction in an uninspiring contest, were somewhat cheered in the twenty-fourth round. Oliver nipped in smartly, landed a hard punch to the face, and cleverly avoided his opponent's attempted blows. The round ended with Donnelly dropping to his knees. 'Now, Tom,' advised the nobleman who was Oliver's patron, 'go to work, my boy, and you cannot lose it.'

Donnelly appeared at 'the scratch' with his face much bloodied. His seconds had been unable to stem the flow from his damaged mouth. Oliver scored to the body and skipped away from Dan's wild attempts to nail him. Both landed to the head, but it was the Irishman who went down, to thunderous cheers from the English supporters. Cribb, Oliver's cornerman, shouted: 'I'll bet a guinea to half a crown on my man.' The current odds were two to one on Oliver.

There was obvious concern in the Irish corner and little to cheer those who had made the trip from Ireland. 'The Battersea Gardener' was well on top now and looked a certain winner. He smartly evaded the ponderous attempts of an increasingly frustrated Donnelly while landing with his own solid shots. His constant grinning annoyed the Irish champion even more and Dan showed signs of losing his temper, a fatal error for any boxer. He recklessly charged at his tormentor, only to run into a couple of hard counters that dropped him to the ground. Donnelly appeared very weak when the pair toed the line for round twenty-seven. Inquirers were told by his seconds that his distressed condition was due to drinking too much water during the intervals. In truth, he was paying the penalty for his inadequate preparation and his careless way of life. The round climaxed with both men tumbling down, Donnelly on top. The Irish fans watched in silence as their idol was knocked down in the twenty-eighth round.

Dan rallied bravely in the next, but as the contestants broke from a clinch, Oliver struck a heavy blow to the Irishman's much-bloodied mouth. Donnelly hit back with a good left of his own that stunned Oliver and 'almost put him in want of a dentist', observed Pierce Egan in *Boxiana*.

Oliver got the better of it in a throw and landed uppermost. One hour had elapsed when the pugilists squared up for round thirty. Donnelly, who had won the admiration of the English fans for his courage, countered a heavy blow with a sharp left to Oliver's face, which momentarily removed his grin. They swapped punches evenly until they went down in a tangle, again with Oliver on top.

Donnelly seemed to find new reserves of energy in the thirty-first round and knocked his rival off his feet with a tremendous left swing. He put so much weight behind the blow that the momentum almost brought him down too. 'Dan's wind now seemed improved,' reported Egan, 'and the glint of fire had returned to his eye.'

His confidence growing with his newly found strength, Donnelly sent the Englishman reeling with a smash to the mouth. Oliver, however, was living up to his reputation as 'the bravest of the brave'. He seemed prepared to take everything that was thrown at him. 'You might as well be hitting a tree trunk, Donnelly,' shouted Shelton from Oliver's corner. After an exchange of blows, Oliver, in turning to avoid a heavy swing, slipped to the turf. Donnelly, unable to check his advance, fell over him. 'Haven't you a right hand, Dan?' inquired Tom Belcher when Dan rested on his knee during the break. 'You must use it now if we are to win.'

Donnelly, heeding the advice, crashed home a right to the face, with no reply from his now-feeble opponent. 'Again,' yelled Belcher. Dan obliged. 'That's the way, my boy,' came the enthusiastic response. Oliver grabbed the

Irishman as he sank to the ground, bringing Dan with him. The battle was almost over.

The thirty-fourth round proved to be the last, mercifully for the badly beaten Englishman. He gamely stuck a left into Donnelly's stomach, then pinned Dan's arms as they clinched. Donnelly, unable to break free, butted his opponent in the face. As Tom staggered backwards, Donnelly followed up with a tremendous right to the ear and then threw Tom down with a mighty cross-buttock. Oliver was picked up by his seconds. His head hung limply on his shoulder 'as if it had been disconnected'. Frantic efforts were made to revive him in the half-minute interval, but it was all in vain. He could fight no more. Oliver was still unconscious when 'Time' was called. The battle had lasted one hour and ten minutes.

The cross-buttock, a common manoeuvre in bare-knuckle boxing, was used to good effect by Donnelly in his 1819 encounter with Tom Oliver.

Donnelly, declared the winner to ecstatic cheers from his supporters, strode arm-in-arm with his seconds to a nearby farmhouse to rest, while a doctor attended his beaten rival in an adjoining room. Dan expressed concern about Oliver's condition and was relieved when told he had regained his senses. Before going to console the Englishman, Donnelly thoughtfully concealed Oliver's blue handkerchief beneath his own green one. It was customary to flaunt a defeated man's silk, but the Irish champion had no wish to add to his victim's distress. For all his faults, he had his sensitive side and always displayed consideration for the less fortunate. Oliver, now recovered, took Dan's outstretched hand and the two rivals, who for over an hour had battled with all the strength they could muster, adjourned to a local tavern and drank each other's health. Dan then excused himself to return to the ringside and watch a supporting bout between Lashbrook and Dowd. He had a bet lodged on the result. Later, a barouche and four conveyed him back to the training camp at Riddlesdown, where he spent the night.

The celebrations began in London the following day. Boxers, backers and members of The Fancy spent the hours drinking, dancing and merry-making at Dignam's tavern, the Red Lion, in Clare Market. Donnelly was delighted to welcome Oliver to the party and the two men soon put all thoughts of their grim battle firmly behind them.

'Donnelly's Sprig of Shillelagh', composed by an anonymous Irishman, was sung to loud and prolonged applause:

Crawley Common's the place, and who chanced to
 be there
Saw an Irishman all in his glory appear
With his sprig of shillelagh and shamrock so green.
When in sweet Dublin city he first saw the light,
The midwife he kick'd put the nurse in a fright,
But, said they, upon viewing him belly and back
'He's the boy that will serve them all out with a whack
From his sprig of shillelagh and shamrock so green.'
He thought about fighting before he could talk
And instead of a go-cart, he first learn'd to walk
With his sprig of shillelagh and shamrock so green.
George's Quay was his school, the right place for
 good breeding,
Where the boys mind their stops if they don't mind
 their reading;
There Dan often studied from morning till dark
And he could write, but for shortness, like making
 his mark
With his sprig of shillelagh and shamrock so green.
At his trade, as a chip, he was choice in his stuff,
None pleased him but what was hard, knotty and
 tough
Like his sprig of shillelagh and shamrock so green.
Nor to strip for his work would he ever refuse
And right hand and left, he the mallet could use;
Length and distance could measure without any tool
But his sprig of shillelagh and shamrock so green.
Whenever he arrogance happen'd to meet

No matter in whom, he took out his conceit
With his sprig of shillelagh and shamrock so green.
To the best of all nations that cross'd Dublin bar
Dan was ready at tipping a mill or a spar,
The hot-headed Welshmen served out by the lot
And cut up their leeks small enough for the pot
With his sprig of shillelagh and shamrock so green.
Hall and Cooper went over with wonderful haste
On the soil where it grew, they were longing to taste
Of the sprig of shillelagh and shamrock so green.
On the plains of Kildare 'twas proposed they should
  meet
And Donnelly wished to give them both a good treat;
Yet to such things as Hall, gallant Dan never stoop'd
But he took the stout Cooper, and Cooper well hoop'd
With his sprig of shillelagh and shamrock so green.
And as Irishmen always politeness are taught,
He the visit return'd and to England he brought
His neat sprig of shillelagh and shamrock so green.
With the good-natured stranger the English seem'd
  shy
And Cooper no more fickle fortune would try;
But at last the game Oliver entered the field
And, tho' on his own soil, was soon forced to yield
To the sprig of shillelagh and shamrock so green.
With his kind English friends, he'll again just to
  please 'em
Soon meet, and if troubled with money, soon lose 'em
With his sprig of shillelagh and shamrock so green.

But if John Bull is wise, he'll from market hang back
And keep all the corn he has got in his sack
As to him the next season no harvest will bring
For, like hail, Dan will beat down the blossoms of
  Spring
With his sprig of shillelagh and shamrock so green.

TEN

Paying the Penalty

Donnelly's standing as a prizefighter was now a great topic among The Fancy. The Irish were more convinced than ever that he could beat any man in the world. The English, having finally seen how well he performed in a proper contest, were somewhat less enthused. Many expressed the opinion that he had been much over-rated by the fanciful Irish.

Pierce Egan gave his assessment in *Boxiana*:

The Irish champion has not turned out as good a fighter as was anticipated. He is not the decisive, tremendous hitter with the right as calculated. Had he used it earlier, it would probably have ended in half an hour. He is not lacking in gameness and coolness and is a dangerous man in a fall. Donnelly admitted it was a bad fight, that he acted like a wooden man and could not account for it. He frequently hit with an open right hand. He showed little sign of the punishment taken, except that his right ear was slightly marked and his body was reddened and bruised.

Pierce Egan, author of Boxiana, *was recognized as the foremost authority on the bare-knuckle prize ring. From a drawing by George Sharples.*

There was much speculation as to why he failed to make better use of his vaunted right hand. Some suggested he used it sparingly in order to boost the odds on Oliver and then, when the price was right, he brought the right into play to finish the job. Others thought he hurt the hand in an early round and did not employ it until he knew his rival was ready to be finished off. Donnelly himself offered no excuses. He was clearly disappointed with his showing, especially as he had wanted to impress the sceptical English, but he adamantly rejected suggestions that his unconventional lifestyle had anything to do with it.

Pierce Egan was in no doubt that it was Donnelly's escapades as a 'petticoat poacher' that largely accounted for his 'distressed and blown state' in the latter stages of the fight. It took a doctor's examination to finally bring home to the devil-may-care Irishman the folly of his ways. He was told that he had a venereal disease. Or as Egan, in his eloquent style, put it: 'It is a well known fact that, after his battle with Oliver, it was not only discovered, but Donnelly acknowledged, that he had unfortunately contracted a disease in the promiscuousness of his amours.'

Dan's fall was due mainly to his ignorance of London's temptations, suggested W. Buchanan-Taylor in his book *What Do You Know About Boxing?*

London night life and the 'hells' of St James's put a quick end to the Irish champion's career. He stepped on a toboggan of good living and bad company. The 'hells' referred to were a series of nightclubs of the period; worse, indeed, than the most evil of the night haunts of recent years. One of the things missing was the knowledge of hygiene. The total ignorance of Donnelly aided the acquisition of a disability that laid him low. Yet he was still a hero – possibly a victim of ignorance and, far worse, an amateur in regard to pseudo-love. Donnelly could not 'take it' as we now know the phrase.

Such scandalous news travelled fast, even in the early nineteenth century. Back in Dublin, Dan's wife took the disclosure calmly and rationally. A paragon of understanding, she blamed her husband's situation on the temptations of London. She had opposed the idea of his going to England in the first place, but accepted that it was the only way to pay off his heavy debts. While it was suggested that Mrs Donnelly should have taken a firmer line with her wayward husband, it had to be acknowledged that Dan rarely yielded to any form of discipline, in his sporting or everyday life. Nevertheless, Mrs Donnelly decided she should make the journey to England to have a heart-to-heart talk with her man.

Dan was enjoying the company of members of The Fancy at Tom Belcher's place, the Castle Tavern in Holborn, when a porter informed him that Mrs Donnelly had arrived in London and had taken a room at The White Horse, in Fetter Lane, off Fleet Street. The Irish champion was in a merry mood and kidded the messenger: 'What sort of a woman is it who wants to see me? Is she a big woman, a good-looking woman?' The surprised porter replied: 'Why, sir, don't you know your own wife?' Grinning hugely, Donnelly rose to his feet. 'Never mind,' he said, 'I'll come and have a look at her and see if I know her.'

His wife was asleep in her room when Dan arrived at the inn. She was startled when the curtains around her bed were drawn back and she saw Dan standing there. 'Oh, Dan, is that you?' she inquired. 'You look so pale I hardly recognize you.' He scolded her for following him over to

England: 'Did you think I was dead? Have you brought over my coffin?'

After arguing over what she had heard about his behaviour, Mrs Donnelly could see it was useless trying to get him to change his ways. She did gain one important concession from him. He agreed that she would stay with him as long as he remained in England. Her loyalty and devotion, especially when he was taking frequent detours off the 'straight and narrow' for drinking binges and to play around with other women, seems remarkable. As for Dan, he seemed unable – or unwilling – to resist the slightest temptation. Yet he would always turn to his wife in moments of torment or remorse.

Nowhere in the publications of the period was Mrs Donnelly's first name mentioned, or how many children the couple had. Only *Blackwood's Magazine*, in its May 1820 issue, three months after Donnelly's death, referred to 'his beloved Rebecca' and 'his sons', but its editor, Professor John Wilson, was notoriously given to flights of fancy in his writings. Under the pen name of 'Christopher North', he referred in glowing terms to the Irish champion's virtues:

> The domestic life of Sir Daniel was marked by all the most endearing features that characterize the tender husband, the fond father, the sincere, the generous friend. Early in life he formed a connection with an amiable and enlightened female of the Society of Friends [Quakers] who was the balm of every wound in life, the soft and pleasing pillow upon which he reclined his head in the awful hour of death.

Meanwhile, as Donnelly's reputation as a prizefighter to be feared diminished following his below-par showing against Oliver, challenges poured in from boxers who had hitherto sought to avoid him. On 14 August 1819, the following notice appeared in London's *Weekly Dispatch*: 'A challenge to Dan Donnelly, the conqueror of Oliver. I, the undersigned, do hereby offer to fight you for 1,000 guineas at any place and at any time which may be agreeable to you, provided it be in England. Signed: Enos Cope, innkeeper, Macclesfield.'

A nobleman offered Donnelly his choice of opponent from George Cooper, Bob Gregson, Harry Sutton, Tom Spring, Jack Carter, Bill Neat, Bill Richmond and Ned Painter for a match at £100-a-side. Dan rejected all challengers. His followers were not made aware of it, but he seemed to have made up his mind to turn his back on the sport that had brought him fame. He was reluctant to even talk about boxing. Especially when in the company of members of The Fancy, he would try to steer the conversation away from pugilism, though not always successfully. His growing aversion to being seen as a prizefighter, and nothing else, was typified one night as he dined at one of his favourite taverns, the Red Lion, in Clare Market. Word reached him that a group of Irishmen was downstairs in the Long Room and wished to meet him and shake his hand. Donnelly, angered at what he regarded as an intrusion, shouted: 'Sure what do they take me for – a beast that is to be made a show of? I am no fighting man and I will not exhibit myself to please anybody.' His companions, at length, managed to calm him down and persuade him that it would be impolite not to accede to such a simple request. He went downstairs and entered the Long Room to loud cheers from his delighted fans.

London life was grand as long as the means was there to sustain it, but Dan's financial state was in rapid decline due to his ring inactivity and his many extravagances. Gambling was another of his vices. His luck was certainly out on a visit to one of the West End's most notorious 'hells' in a bid to recoup some of his squandered earnings. It was 'a great secret, only whispered all over London', that he lost £80 in one disastrous night's gambling, said one report. Acting as if the banknotes were falling, along with the autumn leaves, from the trees in Hyde Park, Donnelly could be found nearly every day and night in one tavern or another. Mrs Donnelly did not share her husband's enthusiasm for the metropolis and managed to persuade him to return to Ireland. Dan hit on an idea to make some money at the annual Donnybrook Fair, which was coming up soon. He convinced two English boxers, Bob Gregson and George Cooper, his former foe and now his friend, to accompany him and put on sparring exhibitions in Donnelly's boxing booth.

Dan had just £20 in his pocket as he waited for the stagecoach to take him to Liverpool, where he would catch the boat to Dublin. It was all he had to show for over six months spent in England, but even that amount was about to be severely watered down. Just as he was about to board the coach, a bailiff handed him a writ ordering him to pay

£18 to his old friend and sparmate Jack Carter. 'By the powers,' exclaimed Donnelly, 'it is the other way around. Carter is indebted to me.' He told the lawman his side of the story. The last time he had met Carter was on 27 May, the second day of the Epsom races, when the drunken Englishman had paraded around the racecourse trying to goad him into a fight and vowing he would beat him, either in Ireland or England. Dan said he had accepted the challenge and put down a £2-deposit for the fight to be staged within a month for £500-a-side, or there and then if Carter so desired. Neither Carter nor the £2 had he seen since. He vehemently denied that Carter had later deposited £18 and that he (Donnelly) had ducked out of the agreement. It was he who should be suing Carter, he insisted. The bailiff sympathized with Donnelly's position, but said he could not withdraw the writ. Dan saw he had no option but to pay up. If he stayed in London to contest the issue, he would not alone forfeit the boat fare for his wife and himself, but he would also miss the chance to appear at Donnybrook Fair. In a great rage, he discharged the writ and ordered the coach driver to proceed at a gallop. All that was left of the proceeds of his entire English venture was a measly £2.

ELEVEN

The Prince Regent and 'Sir Daniel'

Our worthy Regent was so delighted
With the great valour he did evince
That Dan was cited, aye, and invited
To 'Come be knighted' by his own Prince.

Truly the most fanciful of the many legends attached to Dan Donnelly is that he was granted a knighthood by the Prince Regent (later King George IV). It is said that, on being introduced to the boxer, the Regent remarked: 'I am glad to meet the best fighting man in Ireland.' To which the brash Donnelly replied: 'I am not that, your Royal Highness, but I am the best in England.' The prince laughed heartily and took so immediate a liking to the Irishman that, so the story goes, he bestowed upon him the honour of a knighthood.

The Prince Regent, later King George IV, allegedly awarded a knighthood to Donnelly, but there is no verification of the legend of 'Sir Daniel'. Copy of an oil painting by John Hoppner, 1807. Courtesy Walker Art Gallery, Liverpool.

Unfortunately, there is no evidence to confirm the laying of the sword on Dan's broad shoulders. There is no doubt that Donnelly, either for egotistical reasons or to extend a practical joke, asserted his right to be called 'Sir Daniel'. And rare was the Irishman of the period who dared to doubt his word. Most of the poems and other written tributes published after his death referred to him as 'Sir Daniel', but it is noticeable that neither the inscription on his tombstone in Kilmainham nor that on the monument in Donnelly's Hollow paid him any such honour. Among the pugilistic scribes of the time, only Pierce Egan, the editor of *Boxiana*, appears to have lent any support to the legend. But even Egan, who professed to be 'a great advocate of data', confessed he did not witness the event. As he 'did not doubt the honour or courage of the fighting hero', Egan said that he 'took it for granted that Donnelly received the knighthood … and that it was an honorary thing altogether, without any tip being demanded'.

Another source claimed that it was 'a wild Irish peer' who delivered Dan's knighthood on the Regent's behalf. Harold Furniss, editor of *Famous Fights*, a British weekly publication that ran from 1901 to 1904, affirmed his belief that Lord Coleraine (George Hanger), an eccentric dandy and close friend of the Prince, had performed the deed, but that he did so 'during a drunken orgy' and the knighthood was a 'mockery'. When he tried to express this view to some Irish supporters of Donnelly, Furniss said he was howled down. 'I daresay that there are still some ignorant Irishmen living who hold that belief,' he concluded, 'and it only shows what a halo of romance and legend surrounds the name of Dan Donnelly and everything connected with him.'

Donnelly's alleged personal account of the knighthood was published in *The Mirror of Literature, Amusement and Instruction* on 19 September 1829. According to the unnamed author, Dan claimed that the knighting ceremony took place at Carlton House, the Prince Regent's mansion in Pall Mall, London. The writer claimed he was a friend of 'the great man', who had gone to his rescue when he was attacked by a gang at Donnybrook Fair. 'Dan rushed from his tent to show fair play and, in an instant, my cowardly assailants fled as if scattered by a whirlwind,' he recalled. During the fair, Donnelly could usually be found in the midst of 'wondering listeners' as he recounted his 'extraordinary adventures'. The crowd would take in every word 'as if it was heresy to doubt him for an instant', observed the writer, 'though my love of truth obliges me to confess that one or two stories I have heard him relate sounded a little apocryphal'.

In the article, under the headline 'Sir Dan Dann'ly, the Irish Haroe', the pugilist is quoted in the most outrageous of Irish brogues, allegedly informing the Regent's messenger: 'Tell his honour I'll be wid him in the twinklin' ov a bedpost, the minit I take my face from behind me beard, and get on me clane flax.' Given directions on arrival at the main entrance to Carlton House, Dan made his way across the yard where 'soldiers marched, fiddlers played, monkeys danced, and there was every kind of diversion', until he reached the royal drawing room. There he found the Regent sitting on his throne and wearing his crown 'with half a hundredweight of gold in it'. After exchanging pleasantries, the prince handed Dan a glass of Irish whiskey and surprised him by suggesting they spar together. Donnelly expressed the fear that he might cause him harm, but was instructed to 'do your worst, Dan, and devil may care'. They commenced to spar and, after some harmless exchanges, the Irishman let fly with a punch that caught his host beneath the ear and sent him tumbling onto his throne. Far from being upset, the Regent said: 'I'm none the worse of the fall and I'm not able for you.' A relieved Donnelly complimented his regal sparring partner on his efforts, assuring him that 'if I had you in training for six months, I'd make another man of you'. After taking a few more whiskeys together, Dan obeyed the command to kneel down, whereupon the prince proclaimed: 'You went down on your knees as plain Dan, but I give you leave to rise as Sir Daniel Donnelly.'

It is a good yarn, to be sure, and it is easy to imagine Dan getting a great kick out of relating it to all who were prepared to listen. Whether one is prepared to accept its authenticity is quite another thing. Even the venue of the alleged knighting ceremony varies considerably in the written accounts. Nat Fleischer's *Ring Record Book* suggested that the honour was conferred at a banquet given by the Lord Lieutenant of Ireland (First Earl Talbot of Hensol) in Donnelly's honour. It is possible that the viceroy performed the deed at the monarch's command, but again there is nothing in the official records to confirm it. Certainly, the Prince Regent was not present at the banquet, for he did not visit Ireland until 1821, the year after Donnelly's death. This also serves to discount the story that the Regent visited Dan at one of his Dublin taverns and 'was so impressed by the Irish champion's phenomenal bravery and manliness that he knighted him on the spot'.

So if prince and pugilist ever met, it has to have been in England. Some contemporary reports claimed that the Regent was present at the fight between Donnelly and Oliver and that the conferring of the knighthood took place at the Irishman's celebration party. This, too, seems highly unlikely. The prince, though an ardent supporter of prizefighting, had not attended a contest since he witnessed the brutal battle between his chairman, or sedan carrier, Tom Tyne and a fighter named Earl at Brighton in 1788. Earl died as a result of the beating he took and, due to the resultant outcry, the prince publicly announced his disassociation from the sport, though secretly maintaining his interest. That Donnelly and the Regent met socially is not beyond the bounds of possibility. The Irish champion was regularly invited to banquets and gatherings of the nobility, where his charm and ready wit made him a popular guest. Among his admirers was said to be Lord Byron. A keen boxing fan, Byron, though handicapped with a foot deformity, had been an earnest pupil of 'Gentleman' John Jackson, the former champion of England. The celebrated poet often sparred with Jackson, whom he termed 'the Professor of Pugilism', at his boxing academy at 13 Bond

Street, London. However, Byron and Donnelly never met. The so-called 'patron saint of romanticism and revolutionary liberalism' left England for good in 1816, three years before Donnelly set foot on English soil. Nor did Dan ever venture further abroad than Britain. If Byron did follow the Irishman's adventures, he did so from Italy. In 1819, while Donnelly was occasionally taking life seriously in England, Byron was living in Ravenna with his mistress, Countess Guiccoli, and developing an interest in Italian revolutionary politics. He was living in Greece, where he sought to aid that country's fight for independence, when he contracted a fever and died in 1824.

An amusing story, though unverified, was told of the day Donnelly met the Duke of Clarence (later King William IV) at the Castle Tavern in Holborn, London. The pub was being run by Tom Spring, who agreed to introduce Dan to the duke. Concerned that 'the uncouth son of Erin' might commit some terrible breach of etiquette, Spring proceed to give him some tips on matters of conduct. 'When you address the duke, always begin by saying Your Grace', he advised. When, a few days later, the Irish champion was introduced to the duke, he made a low and awkward bow, then said: 'For what I am about to receive, O Lord, make me truly thankful.' To which the smiling duke replied 'Amen' and slipped a guinea into Dan's hand. Later, Tom Spring remonstrated with Donnelly for asking the duke for money. 'But sure I didn't ask him for a penny,' protested Dan. 'You told me to say your grace and that is all I did.'

The Prince Regent's admiration for boxers stemmed from the cult of manliness that prevailed in the period. He shared the popular conception of pugilists as the true epitome of manly virtue and he despised homosexuals. This was not to say that the Regent's association with prize-fighters won him any plaudits from the general public. His heavy drinking, loose morals and wild extravagances at a time of economic hardship had already assured him of widespread unpopularity. Regardless of what his subjects thought of the idea, he chose to engage eighteen of England's leading boxers as bodyguards for his coronation as George IV in July 1821. Their role was to protect the monarch from possible attack as the royal procession wound its way through the crowded London streets and later, if required, to act as 'chuckers out' of uninvited guests at the ceremony. Among the pugilists hired for the occasion were Donnelly's last opponent, Tom Oliver, along with the Irish champion's former sparmates and associates, Jack Carter, Tom Spring, Tom Belcher, Bill Richmond, Ben Burns and Harry Harmer, as well as the English champion, Tom Cribb. Donnelly himself might well have been included had he not died the previous year. The use of the boxers by the new king was condemned as the act of a frightened bully, but George IV was so pleased that he ordered the Lord Chamberlain to send a letter of thanks to each man. He also had a golden coronation medal specially cast for them. It was later raffled and won by Tom Belcher.

But for all his fondness for the fistic breed, can it really be accepted that the only boxer he honoured with a knighthood was Dan Donnelly? Is it feasible that an Irishman should have been the chosen one above renowned English champions like Cribb and Spring? Indeed, it was not until 2000 that Henry Cooper, the former British, British Empire and European heavyweight champion, became the first official boxing knight. In some support of the Donnelly legend, it is a fact that George IV showed a warm affection towards the Irish. He always felt at ease in their company and professed to a sympathetic understanding of most of the country's problems. Consequently, he was more popular with the Irish than he was at home. A measure of his depth of feeling for his Irish subjects was the fact that he chose Ireland as the first place to visit after his coronation. No reigning British sovereign had set foot in Ireland since the time of Richard II. As the procession wound its way through the centre of Dublin, the king, wearing the Order of St Patrick sash on his field marshal's uniform, stood up in his open carriage waving his hat, pointing to the huge bunch of shamrock attached to it, and laying his hand on his heart, acknowledged the cheers of the dense throng. He charmed the people with his friendliness and approachability, with the easy way he shook them by the hand, talked to them and smiled at them. One elderly Dubliner, voicing a common sentiment, remarked: 'I was a rebel to old King George III, but by God I'd die a thousand deaths for his son, because he's a real king and asks us how we are.'

A valiant attempt to explain the legend of Donnelly's knighthood was made by Pierce Egan, the London-born son of an Irish migrant paviour, whose quaint writing style, despite its eccentric overuse of capital letters, italics and slang words, qualifies him as the supreme chronicler of the bare-knuckle prize ring. His *Boxiana*, published in five volumes between 1812 and 1829, is regarded as a masterpiece of sporting literature. In volume three, Egan refers to 'Sir Daniel' as a 'Knight of the Most Ancient Order of the Fives', and goes on:

> This Order takes the precedence of all others. It is an act of nature and was acknowledged in estimation before the existence and authority of kings and emperors. The use of the 'fives' originated with Ould Adam, and Eve also had a 'finger' in it, and it was handed down from generation to generation. It also proved of most essential to Saint Patrick in carrying his cross to Ireland. In the revival of the Order of the Fives then, in the person of the champion of Ireland, by his royal highness the Prince Regent, the warm-hearted and generous people of Ireland applauded this heroic act to the skies.

If any real sense is to be made of Egan's account, it would appear to suggest that Donnelly was honoured for his skill with his hands, the mythical 'Order of the Fives' being restricted to those who could use their hands to advantage. Nowadays, the closed fist is often referred to as a 'bunch of fives'.

The legend of the Prince Regent elevating Ireland's prizefighting hero to the rank of 'Sir' is fully in keeping with the period, one of the most romantic, extravagant and wildly contrasting in English history. It produced more than its fair share of extraordinary characters, none more

Boxiana, *published in five parts between 1812 and 1829, was an indispensable guide for followers of pugilism.*

complex than the Regent himself. An overweight, vain 'spoilt child', he squandered enormous sums of money on satisfying his frequent whims to change the entire structure and décor of his many residences. He even altered his birthday because the date did not suit him. 'The Regency was comparatively brief but had a character, a tone, a tang, all its own,' observed J.B. Priestly in *The Prince of Pleasure and his Regency 1811–20*. Priestly brilliantly described the great contrasts of attitudes, of behaviour, of conditions, and the larger than life personalities of the period.

> Down one side of the street may be seen the evangelicals, the prigs and the prudes, and down the other go the gamesters, the extravagant dandies, the drunken womanisers … the age swings between extremes of elegance and refinement and depths of sodden brutality and misery. It has no common belief, no accepted code, no general standard of conformity. It seems horrible one moment, enchanting the next.
>
> Anything and everything can be happening. In the North [of England] some men are inventing and setting up new machines while other men are going by night with huge hammers to break them. Wellington is having fifty men flogged while Wordsworth is gazing at a celandine. Jane Austen is sending Mansfield Park to her publishers; Lady Caroline Lamb is sending Lord Byron clippings of pubic hair. Wilberforce is denouncing the slave trade while Beau Brummell is denouncing with equal gravity an imperfectly-tied cravat.
>
> In a city [London] where many people think it is wicked to row a boat on Sunday, young noblemen lose £25,000 in a night at Waiter's, tiny boys of six are forced up chimneys, prostitutes of fourteen roam the streets. Down at Brighton, in his fantastic Pavilion, the Regent is believed to be staging wild orgies, perhaps with kid-

napped virgins, when in fact, with his stays loosened over the curacao, he is giving imitations of cabinet ministers to amuse the grandmothers who are his favourites. All appearances tend to be deceptive; too many public personages are either drunk or a trifle cracked …

One anonymous poet had no doubt as to where Donnelly ranked among the great men of battle when he penned these lines:

Ye may prate of your Wellingtons, Bluchers and Neys,
And smother them over with blarney and praise,
But greater than all was the Knight of the Fist,
Who bate all the boxers he met on the list,
Sir Dan Donnelly.

A drawing of Dan Donnelly, engraved by H. Brocas and published by M. Sandford, of 45 Henry Street, Dublin, that failed to capture a true likeness.

TWELVE

Donnybrook Fair

Whether they recognized him as 'Sir Daniel' or not, the Irish gave Donnelly a welcome befitting a king on his return from England. Thousands of excited men, women and children – rich and poor alike – lined the quays as the packet steamer docked at the Pigeon House after its twenty-three hour journey from Liverpool. Cries of 'Welcome home, Dan' and 'Donnelly forever' echoed across Dublin Bay.

He had expected a warm reception, but nothing of this magnitude. People had waited for hours to greet him and minor skirmishes broke out among those striving to touch him. A white horse had been kept in readiness to carry the conquering hero through the main streets of the capital, and Dan laughed heartily as a couple of brawny men hoisted him onto the animal's back. So many people were gathered at Townsend Street, the Irish champion's birth-place, that the procession was forced to a halt. Donnelly expressed his gratitude to the people for their warm recep-tion and, with a parting flourish of his mighty right arm, he dismounted and retired to a local tavern to drink a toast to their health. As many of his supporters as could cram into the premises joined in the festivities, which continued into the following morning.

Donnybrook Fair opened on 27 August 1819. The world-famous event had been staged annually for over 600 years and, for the two weeks it lasted, it was invariably the scene of wild merrymaking and regular drunken brawls. Various sideshows included 'horse tumbling, sleight of hand, serious and comic singing and the music of the bag-pipes and fiddle'. But the real fun was to be found at night, when things really got swinging. Alongside the many attrac-tions, the festivities often deteriorated into fights in which fists, sticks and bottles were flung with wild abandon. It was no wonder that the term 'a donnybrook' grew into popular usage to describe a free-for-all brawl. Clearly, Donnybrook Fair was no place for any self-respecting female to be seen. Taking account of the number of 'painted prostitutes, drunken youths and lassies' to be found there, the *Dublin Penny Journal* ventured to say that 'there is more misery and madness, devilment and debauchery than could be found crowded into any equal space of ground in any part of this globe. It has been calculated that during the period of Donnybrook Fair there is more loss of female character and greater spoliation of female virtue among the lower orders than during all other portions of the year'.

The main attraction at Donnybrook Fair in 1819 was undoubtedly Donnelly's boxing booth. The tents housing the various sideshows were made up of sticks and sods of turf covered with old sheets, petticoats and rags. Inside, benches were installed along the sides for customers to witness the presentations. In the boxing booth, a ten-foot ring was erected and, for a modest fee, visitors were invited to watch the Irish champion in exhibitions with his two English sparring partners, George Cooper and Bob Gregson. A ballad was composed especially for the fair and was printed on paper sheets so the audiences could join in. Entitled 'Donnybrook Fair', it gave a pretty good description of the event. Sung to the air of 'Robin Adair', it went as follows:

> What made the town so dull?
> Donnybrook Fair.
> What made the tents so full?
> Donnybrook Fair.
> Where was the joyous ground,
> Booth, tent and merry-ground?
> Donnybrook Fair.
>
> Beef, mutton, lamb and veal,
> Donnybrook Fair.
> Wine, cider, porter, ale,
> Donnybrook Fair.

Whiskey, both choice and pure,
Men and maids most demure,
Dancing on the ground flure,
Donnybrook Fair.
Where was the modest bow?
Donnybrook Fair.
Where was the friendly row?
Donnybrook Fair.
Where was the gay resort?
Where Sir Dan held his court,
Donnybrook Fair.

Donnybrook Fair, as depicted in this 1830 print (unattributed), was the annual scene of unruly behaviour, with beggars, drunks, gamblers, prostitutes, and stick-fighters all competing for attention alongside the various sideshows, improvised shops and drinking tents.

For the first few days of the fair, the crowds flocked to the boxing booth. They were disappointed to find Donnelly refusing to take the sparring matches seriously. He laughed, joked and clowned throughout most of his appearances and 'only occasionally demonstrated how things might be done in the ring'. Much of the blame was laid on Dan's adoring followers who, according to a contemporary journal, 'constantly gave him drops of the cratur and thus prevented him from exerting himself'. Very often Dan, suffering from an outsized hangover, failed to show up for his billed appearances. As a result, most of the boxing was left to Cooper and Gregson. The scientific ability of Cooper, still remembered with affection by the Irish for his courageous losing battle against Donnelly at the Curragh four years earlier, was especially appreciated by the spectators. However, it was the Irish champion they had paid to see and they were not slow to voice their disapproval of his absences. When word got around that Donnelly's appearances could not be guaranteed, attendances at the boxing booth fell away. So what had looked like being a lucrative fortnight for the three pugilists was close to being a flop, thanks to Donnelly's failure to stay sober for even that long.

Another sour note was introduced when Jack Carter turned up at the fair. For several days, in a drunken stupor, he staggered around from tent to tent looking for Donnelly and calling for a fight. 'The Lancashire Hero', whose action in having a writ served on Dan had earned him few admirers, even among the English, had followed

Donnelly to Ireland to further annoy him. Carter's obnoxious behaviour went largely unnoticed at the fair, where such carry-on was viewed as quite normal. So rowdy was the annual event that a lengthy campaign for its abolition was eventually successful and the last Donnybrook Fair was held in 1855. Though now a respectable Dublin suburb, it took a long time to rid itself of the association with 'merry-making, whiskey drinking and skull cracking'.

Carter continued to pester Donnelly for a fight after the 1819 fair ended. In a letter to the *Dublin Journal* of 18 September, he claimed that Dan had failed to answer his earlier challenge for a match at £200-a-side. Two days later, in the same paper, Carter's allegation was refuted in a letter from 'a committee of friends and supporters of Donnelly'. The group claimed that Dan had accepted the challenge and, furthermore, they had lodged £200 in his support. Arrangements had been made for an interview, they said, but 'neither Carter or his friends, if he has any', had showed up. Parties representing both boxers did ultimately meet at 20 Fownes Street, Dublin, to sign a provisional agreement for a match between Donnelly and Carter. W. Dowling deposited £20 as a guarantee on Donnelly's behalf and L. Byrne did likewise for Carter, with John Dooly entrusted to hold the deposits. Both sides agreed to meet again on 5 October to increase the guarantees to fifty guineas a side. If either of the parties failed to honour the date, it was decided that the original deposits of £20 would be forfeited. The proposed date for the fight was 25 November. It would take place at a venue within thirty miles of Dublin, the exact site to be decided by the toss of a coin. The purse money would be £200.

The news of the proposed match brought delight to Donnelly's vast legion of supporters. Not for four years had a major prizefight been held on Irish soil and they were anxious to see what improvements he had acquired from his spell in England. Carter, a talented performer in the ring, would provide a good test. Alas, they were doomed to disappointment. The fight never took place. Donnelly, when the parties representing both boxers met on 5 October, insisted that he would only meet Carter on a winner-take-all basis and that the total stake money be deposited with a person of his choosing. Carter refused to accept these terms. He recalled that Tom Hall and George Cooper had both complained of unfair treatment when they fought Donnelly on his native turf, and he angrily denounced the Irish champion for not agreeing to a share of the purse. The meeting broke up with each side hurling abuse and accusations of trickery and cowardice at the other. Sadly, Donnelly and Carter, one-time friends and business associates, were to remain bitter antagonists. Neither was blameless for the break-up. Carter's action in suing Donnelly for almost every penny of his English earnings was heartless, and no one could excuse his drunken abuse of the Irish champion during Donnybrook Fair. Donnelly, on the other hand, was not prepared to test his strength and skill against Carter in a genuine prizefight unless the odds were slanted in his favour.

In Donnelly's case, his demand to have things his

own way, even if it meant employing unfair tactics, was in contrast to his normal generous nature. But his stubborn side was shown on another occasion when one of his protégés, Pat Halton, fought Jack Langan on the Curragh. Halton, known as 'Donnelly's Boy', had been taught the art of boxing by Dan and, for a time, he looked likely to emulate his tutor as an Irish champion. He failed to live up to expectations, however, and took a severe beating from Langan, one of the best Irish pugilists of the bare-knuckle era. After an hour of battling, Halton had clearly lost heart and was beaten to the ground by Langan. Donnelly, Halton's chief second, tried desperately to revive his fighter during the half-minute interval without success. Langan, as he was fully entitled to do, claimed the victory. Donnelly, however, got his battered protégé to his feet and demanded that he be allowed to continue the fight. Langan's seconds maintained that their man was the rightful winner because his opponent had failed to toe the line in time, but still Donnelly would not consent to giving him the purse. Angry words were exchanged and the match ended in uproar. Later that evening, Langan traced Donnelly to the Cockpit Inn and remonstrated with him for his unsporting behaviour. Dan had been his idol and it saddened him to be treated this way. The row heightened until Langan shouted bitterly: 'I know, Dan, that you could beat me. Yet I will hold you a wager that you do not lick me in half an hour if we fight right now.' Donnelly rejected the challenge and, after some further argument, he agreed to give Langan the money he was due.

It was obvious by now that Donnelly had lost all desire to fight again, although his fervent fans clung onto the hope that they could persuade him otherwise. Dan, now more than ever, abhorred the rigours of training, such little as he ever did, and could not face the prospect of getting into condition for a fight to the finish. Though outwardly in prime health, he was still not fully rid of the sexually transmitted disease he had contracted in England and he was drinking more heavily than ever. He did not realize, or chose to ignore, the great damage he was causing to his body.

Although the life of a publican was not the ideal occupation for someone with his love of alcohol, Donnelly appeared to finally get his act together. His fourth and last Dublin pub, The Shining Daisy at 29 Pill Lane, was situated at the junction of Pill Lane (now Chancery Street) and Greek Street, at the rear of the Four Courts, and reported a brisk trade. It was especially popular with farmers up from the country to conduct business at the nearby fruit and vegetable market. They took delight in calling at Donnelly's place for the privilege of shaking his hand and drinking his porter. Dan, his fame established, enjoyed nothing more than chatting and joking with his customers and 'drinking his glass dry'. His old friend-turned-foe, Jack Carter, had taken up residence in Dublin and held the licence of The Black Lion in Kilmainham, while Bob Gregson was another boxer-turned-publican in Moore Street. Prizefighting, obviously, was a popular topic in the Irish capital.

Donnelly, banishing forever all thought of a ring comeback, looked to new fields to conquer. His strong personality and gift for public speaking gave him the idea that he might try his hand at politics and campaign for justice for his downtrodden fellow Catholics, a cause very close to his heart. Another Daniel (O'Connell) was struggling for support for his emancipation campaign, but was still some years from seeing at least part of his dream realized. In the meantime, Irish Catholics, though freed from the worst of the Penal Laws, still struggled with injustices like the payment of tithes to the Established (Protestant) Church and the limiting of the vote to owners of freehold property worth over forty shillings (£2). No Catholic could be a Member of Parliament although four-fifths of the population was of that faith. They were also forbidden to hold any public office, even at local level. In 1798, while Donnelly was still at school, the frustration of the people boiled over into a rebellion led by the Society of United Irishmen and inspired by Theobald Wolfe Tone and Lord Edward Fitzgerald. The rising was savagely suppressed and resulted in the deaths of Tone and Fitzgerald among many others. An unsuccessful attempt by Robert Emmet to organize a revolt in 1803 spelt the end of the United Irishmen and the mood turned towards political agitation.

In Donnelly, the downtrodden Irish saw not just a champion prizefighter, but also a champion of their cause for justice. By his stirring victories over top-ranked English fighters, he symbolized ultimate success in Ireland's long, bitter fight for freedom from the oppressors. Dan was intensely proud of being Irish and made no apologies for his nationality when the English sought his companionship when he attained fame in the ring. They could take him as he was or not at all.

He had no time for those who brought shame on his native land. On one occasion, someone was rash enough to suggest that Peter Corcoran was a better Irish fighter. Donnelly angrily retorted: 'Bloody end to his soul! He sold out his country and that is something I will never do.' Corcoran, the first Irishman to gain recognition as heavyweight champion of England, lost the title to Harry Sellars in a fight that was widely held to be 'fixed'. Corcoran prospered from the alleged 'payoff' but lost the support of the general public, and when he died he had to be buried by subscription.

Donnelly, at any rate, did not pursue his ambition to enter the political arena, probably realizing, or being wisely counselled, that he would face even tougher fighting and risk heavier beatings than ever he took in the prize ring. Lord Byron, apparently, was convinced that the Irish champion would have made an excellent bishop, if not a politician. In Venice, when he heard of the Irish champion's death, the poet allegedly remarked that 'Dan would have been a great man in the pulpit'.

THIRTEEN

The Fatal Knockout

On the morning of 15 February 1820, Dan complained to his wife of feeling dull and heavy. He dismissed it, however, as a trifling cold, probably brought about by a strenuous game of fives the previous day. He had finished the ball game perspiring heavily and drank a large amount of water to cool off. Dan spent a while in his Pill Lane tavern chatting to customers, but found himself short of breath, so he decided to take a walk in the hope that the fresh air would clear his lungs. He had not gone far when he felt himself weakening and returned to the pub. Not wishing to disclose his illness, he joined his customers again, but was forced to excuse himself to go and lie down in bed.

When Mrs Donnelly closed the premises at midnight, she was alarmed to find her husband's condition had worsened considerably. After seeing Dan spending a rest-less night, she sent for a doctor and was shocked when told that he held out little hope for her husband's recovery. She refused to accept that he would succumb to a sudden ill-ness. Wasn't he a man above ordinary mortals? Hadn't he proved his strength and resilience many times in the prize ring? And wasn't it also true that, for all his careless ways, he had never had a serious day's sickness in his life?

Once, he had boasted to an English nobleman who questioned his attitude to training, that 'nothing can hurt me, liquor cannot make me drunk, whiskey has no power over my frame, my arm is like iron, my thigh is as hard as brass, my legs can keep company with the best grey-hounds, and my heart is too big for my body'.

Dan's wife recalled the story he told her of the time when, as an adventurous young man of twenty, he had gone to the north of Ireland seeking work as a carpenter and some enjoyment. Tired and hungry after spending his meagre earnings in various country pubs, he had failed to hitch a lift back to Dublin and spent the night sleeping on a tombstone. He awoke none the worse for his exposure to the chilly night air. And many was the occasion that he staggered home from a pub after closing time in pouring rain and, too drunk to reach his destination, had lain down in a coach-house doorway or on the floor of an uninhab-ited cellar, his body absorbing the dampness of his clothes. On frequent drinking sprees with his friends, he would eat nothing for three or four days, consuming just whiskey and porter. He scorned all well-meant advice to look after his health, stubbornly believing that his God-given strength would resist any illness. It turned out to be a sadly misguided assumption.

Dan slept soundly on the day of the doctor's visit until 11 pm, when he awoke in a state of convulsion. Mrs Donnelly expressed her alarm, but was pacified when he seemed to calm down after a turbulent few hours. The following morning Dan was in great pain and was weakening rapidly. His wife asked him if she should send for a priest. He nodded his consent. The priest administered the Last Rites of the Catholic Church and Dan managed a weak smile of gratitude. Surprisingly, the former Irish champion showed signs of rallying and gave hope that he would be able to withstand Death's knockout blow. Again exhibiting the remarkable powers of recovery that had characterized his ring battles, he felt well enough at midday to ask his son to fetch his clothes so he could go downstairs and join his customers. He managed to dress himself and, resting his arm on his son's shoulder, tried to walk across the bedroom. He only got as far as a couch when he collapsed.

At one o'clock on the morning of 18 February 1820, his head cradled in his sobbing wife's arms, Dan finally gave up the fight. Just before he died, he passed judgment upon himself: 'I have been given so much and I have done so little.'

Pierce Egan, in *Boxiana*, gave his imaginative take on Donnelly's death:

> In the midst of a gay laughing scene, one of the ugliest customers Dan had ever met with introduced himself,

without making any previous match or agreeing as to 'Time' and, cruel to relate, gave the Irish champion such a flooring hit that all the wind in his body was knocked out in a twinkling. He never saw the 'scratch' afterwards and poor Dan closed his ogles for ever upon the prize ring.

The obituary notice in *Carrick's Morning Post* read:

Died, at his porter house in Greek Street, Mr Dan Donnelly, known in the pugilistic school as the Champion of Ireland. It is said that he overheated himself a few days back playing rackets and his death was caused by inflammation of the lungs. He was about forty years of age. His unexpected and rather sudden death will be deeply lamented by the Fancy. The amateurs declare that no other antagonist, save grim Death, could have milled him off the stage. Peace to his manes.

The Freeman's Journal had him a little older and differed in the cause of his death. He was 'in his forty-fourth year' and his passing was 'in consequence of his bursting a blood vessel'. *Saunder's Newsletter* did not mention his age or what might have killed him. The paper reported that there were 'many rumours respecting this individual's sudden death, but, as we have not received any authentic information as yet concerning it, we merely announce the circumstance'. One of the wilder rumours, that Dan's drink had been poisoned by a jealous Englishman, was firmly quashed when a post-mortem revealed that he had died of natural causes, although no cause of death was reported. The suggestion that his habit of drinking large amounts of cold water while perspiring heavily might have led to his demise seems feasible. Donnelly had a makeshift gymnasium at the back of his pub in Pill Lane. Customers who saw him working out with heavy dumbbells and pounding a sawdust-filled sack were often surprised to see him stop to drink several jugs of water before resuming his routine. Sports participants, such as marathon runners, have been known to suffer water intoxication from drinking too much during the course of an event. Water intoxication, also known as hyper-hydration or water poisoning, is a potentially fatal disturbance of brain function that results when the normal balance of electrolytes is pushed outside safe limits by the very rapid intake of water.

Whatever indiscretions he may have committed in his short lifetime, the Irish showed themselves more than willing to forgive their departed hero. Quite astonishing scenes of national mourning followed the announcement of his death. Few popular figures in Irish history were more widely grieved by the common people. On the day of his funeral, shops and other businesses stayed closed as a mark of respect. Theatres, too, suspended their performances. In the Phoenix Park, guns were fired in a salute. As the funeral procession left at 10 am from his last residence, the late champion's gloves rested upon a silk cushion in the hearse. All along the route, crowds lined the streets and many joined the long train of mourners. From all over the country they came, many weeping openly as the flower-bedecked coffin passed through Capel Street, Great Britain Street (now Parnell Street), Sackville Street (now O'Connell

Street) and over Carlisle Bridge (later rebuilt and renamed O'Connell Bridge) to Dan's birthplace in Townsend Street. His unique popularity with the poorer classes was noted by *The Sporting Magazine*, which reported that 'at least 80,000 men, women and children attended the funeral, the roads and streets leading to the burial ground being covered with a moving mass of rags and wretchedness. No tumult or disturbance whatever occurred.'

After leaving College Green, the cortege progressed along Dame Street, Castle Street, Skinners' Row (now Christ Church Place), High Street and Cornmarket into Thomas Street. At this point the horse was unyoked and several of Donnelly's followers proudly pulled the hearse the rest of the way to the burial ground, the Royal Hospital Fields, or Bully's Acre, at Kilmainham. 'Not a sound was heard as the coffin was lowered into the grave save for the lamentations of the family,' noted one newspaper.

A legend exists that Donnelly's remains shared the grave of Prince Murrough, who fell with his father, King Brian Boru, at the Battle of Clontarf in 1014. Murrough was supposed to be buried at the foot of an ancient stone cross, only the stump of which remains. Around 1800 the cross fell and, while being re-erected, a large sword, perhaps owned by Murrough, and a hoard of Danish coins were discovered. The *Dublin Penny Journal* supported the story that the prince's grave was shared with another national hero when, after a lapse of 800 years, it took the remains of Dan Donnelly. 'The victor of Clontarf and the victor of Kildare; the pride of the aristocracy and the idol of the people – they now sleep in the same grave,' said the paper is its issue of 25 August 1832. There is no proof that Murrough was buried in the Bully's Acre, although the fact that the Irish camp was based at Kilmainham before the Battle of Clontarf perhaps lends some credence to the legend. It is untrue, however, that Donnelly's remains lay at the site of the stone cross. In the 1970s, a long-serving groundsman pointed out to this author the spot where older local residents believed Donnelly was buried. A large flat stone, bearing no discernable inscription, covered the grave. No burial records were kept of most of those interred in Bully's Acre. In 1991, many of the remains were exhumed and relocated close by. A new headstone was erected by Dublin Corporation 'to honour those unknown persons who were interred in the nearby Bully's Acre in the distant past'.

Any suggestion that Donnelly was quickly forgotten is certainly without substance. A handsome table-shaped tomb enclosed by railings was erected over his grave, but the memorial, as John Dalton's *The History of County Dublin* explained in 1838, 'is now as extinct as the champion himself'. It had been Dan's dying wish that 'no external pomp shall mark my grave', but his legion of admirers felt that it would be improper to let his memory grow dim without some permanent reminder of the great excitement and pride he had brought them. Two weeks after his death, a committee of twelve was formed at a meeting in Bergin's Great Rooms in Fleet Street, Dublin. The publican, Patrick Bergin, was appointed treasurer, his task being to collect the necessary funds by public subscription for the erection of a memorial. All the publicans throughout the city who had known and admired Donnelly were requested to place collection boxes on their counters. By 1 May, the day the fund closed, a total of £2327 had been raised. The committee considered scores of suggestions for the inscription on the tomb. The chosen epitaph was submitted by Joseph Halliday, inventor of the Royal Kent bugle, or Kent horn, and author of a celebrated pamphlet on Logier's musical system:

> Dan rests beneath, still hold his memory dear,
> Around his tomb let fall the pitying tear;
> Now mingled with his kindred dust he lies
> In silence sleepeth – never more to rise
> Except on that fateful day when all,
> Living and dead, shall hear the trumpet's call.
> Death, Tyrant Death, that fell relentless foe,
> Our champion levell'd by a mortal blow;
> None else in single combat could him harm,
> No human foe resist his mighty arm.
> Erin lament; bear in record his name;
> Lament the man who fought to crown your fame,
> Laid prostrate Cooper, Oliver and Hall,
> Yielding to none but Death, who conquers all.

The initial letter in each line, read downwards, spelled out 'Daniel Donnelly'.

The attractive memorial remained intact for several years until it was targeted and severely damaged by members of a Scottish regiment supposedly on guard duty at the adjacent Royal Hospital. The resultant outrage caused the regiment to be removed from Dublin. In order to safeguard the memorial from further desecration, the wrecked tombstone was removed and, in belated respect to Donnelly's dying wish, a plain unmarked stone was laid in its place.

The fact that Donnelly was buried in Bully's Acre would suggest that he was penniless, or virtually so, at the time of his death. According to Dalton's *The History of County Dublin*, it was the only free graveyard for the city's poor. 'People buried there were unable to meet the burial charges at city churches,' stated the author. The popular name of the burial ground has several suggested origins. One theory is that it got its name because of the number of tough characters buried there. 'Some of those interred there were as alone and friendless in death as in life,' observed one writer. Some historians believe it is a derivative of the Bailli's Acre, named after a high officer of the Knights Hospitallers, whose priory later became the Royal Hospital and is now the Irish Museum of Modern Art. Bully's Acre does have another boxing connection apart from the fact that Dan Donnelly was buried there. The graveyard was once part of the Kilmainham land controlled by John Egan, uncle of Pierce Egan, the author of *Boxiana*. A Member of the Irish Parliament, county court judge and noted duellist, John Egan picked up the nickname of 'Bully' because of his association with Bully's Acre, according to his nephew. A staunch opponent of the Act of Union, 'Bully' delivered an impassioned speech against the proposal when the House had its final debate on the Act. Warned that he would lose the 'chairmanship' of Kilmainham if the Act were passed, he roared: 'Ireland for ever – and damn Kilmainham.' The political merger of Great Britain and Ireland left him in deep depression and he died in poverty in Scotland in 1810.

None of the publications around the time of Donnelly's passing made any mention of his financial state. Nor is there any record of a will he might have made. T.G. Hazard, author of *The Life of Dan Donnelly*, published shortly after the Irish champion's death, maintained that Dan's pub in Pill Lane was doing a brisk trade and 'he was well on his way to making a rapid fortune'. However, Hazard adopted a patronizing approach to his subject and clearly felt obliged to not dwell on such trifles as to how well off he left his grieving family. Although the *Dublin Directory* of 1820 lists 'Daniel Donnelly, vintner, 29 Pill Lane', it is not certain that he actually owned the business. It was common for the proprietors of public houses to install popular figures as landlords with the aim of drawing extra customers. Bearing in mind Donnelly's careless attitude to money, it seems unlikely that he left his family a ready 'nest egg'.

FOURTEEN

But Not Forgotten

If Donnelly, in his lifetime, had achieved the status of a champion, a hero, a demigod, then his premature departure looked like assuring him of immortality. Poets, writers and ballad-composers penned a great profusion of tributes to the departed Irish champion. The journals of the day were full of letters of lamentation and poetic outpourings in homage to his memory.

Typical of the countrywide sense of grievance was the harrowing scenes that marked a meeting of the Cork Philosophical and Literary Society on 22 March, a month after Dan took the fatal count. The guest speaker was Richard Dowden, a Unitarian temperance campaigner and one-time mayor of Cork, who had been a close friend of Donnelly and had taken boxing lessons from him. A full-length transparent painting of the late champion, solemnly draped in black ribbons and lit from behind by six oil lamps, hung on the wall behind the president's chair. The society's artist, Mr Topp, has specially executed it for the occasion.

Tears welled in the eyes of the attentive members as Dowden began his solemn address: 'He, who but a few short days ago was the glory of our land; he, whose intellectual and corporal energies were the theme of every tongue; he, who basked in all the sunshine of prosperity; he, who in all the pride of conscious dignity stood on the loftiest pinnacle of fame and honour; he, whose virtues were as the refreshing dews of Heaven; he – is gone!'

The uncontrollable sobbing of some of the female members, who begged to be excused, momentarily drowned out the speaker's words. The men took advantage of the enforced break to blow into their handkerchiefs and gulp their drinks in attempting to ease the dryness in their throats. Dowden resumed his address: 'The inexorable arm of the King of Terrors has widowed every heart of sensibility. The chilling gloom of despair has frozen every soul. Cribb is glad. Carter rejoices. Hall, Cooper and Oliver are avenged. England triumphs. Donnelly is dead and Erin is no more ...'

One anonymous admirer published *A Monody on the Death of Dan Donnelly* in which he praised the idol's deathbed repentance for his sins. 'From the moment he found himself ill, he presaged death,' the pamphlet related:

Therefore his clergy attended him every hour until he departed. So, thank Heaven, the last conflict was the best, when he fought against despair and the power of darkness, used the shield of faith and sought mercy from the captain of his salvation. What a happy circumstance if those sweet-tongued Christians who boast of their good works would only follow his example.

Pierce Egan's favourite poetic tribute was the following, unsigned, which was published in *Carrick's Morning Post*:

What dire misfortune has our land o'erspread,
Our Irish champion's numbered with the dead;
And he who never did to mortal bend
By Death's cut short and Ireland's lost her Friend.
Ah, cruel Death, why were you so unkind
To take Sir Dan and leave such trash behind
As Gregson, Cooper, Carter, such a clan
To leave behind and take so great a man?
Oh, Erin's daughters, come and shed your tears
On your Champion's grave, who loved you many
    years;
To Erin's sons this day's a day of sorrow;
Who have we now who will defend our Curragh?

Boxiana published this brief lament from an anony-mous Irishman:

Mourn for our champion, snatched away
From the fair Curragh's verdant ring;
Mourn for his fist now wrapped in clay,
No more the ponderous thump to fling.

Blackwood's Magazine devoted no fewer than twenty pages to 'solemn dirges – letters of condolence – lamentations – plaintive ballads – odes – songs – an eloquent philosophical oration – wound up by an advertisement to collect expenses for suitable memorial to be erected to the memory of Ireland's late Champion'. Included were supposed tributes from scholars in Greek, Hebrew and Latin. Language students must have doubted the seriousness of the contributions and have been amused at the licence they took with, for instance, a Latin poem that read, in part:

> Anglorum nunquam cohortem magnanimus in
>   pugna tristi
> Pugilum timuisti (heu ter legende DONNELLE)
> Sed si quis te val Hallus, vel Olivarius, in creparet,
> Vel Cooperus (heu!! etc.)

Lord Byron was alleged to have sent the following poem from Venice. Written in the style of his *Childe Harold*, it was entitled 'Childe Daniel':

> In Fancy-land there is a burst or two,
> The spirits' tribute to the fallen, see
> On each scarr'd front the cloud of sorrow glow,
> Bloating its sprightly shine. But what is he
> For whom grief's mighty butt is broached so free?
> Were his brows shadowed by the awful crown,
> The Bishop's mitre, or high plumery
> Of the Mailed Warrior? Won he his renown
> On pulpit, throne or field, who Death hath now
>   struck down?

Lord Byron (in dressing gown) sparring with 'Gentleman' John Jackson at the former English champion's boxing academy in Bond Street, London. The famous poet was an admirer of Dan Donnelly and thought he would make an excellent bishop. From a print by A. Forbes Sieveking.

He won it in a field where arms are none
Save those the mother gives to us.
He was a climbing star which had not fully shown,
Yet promised in its glory to surpass
Our champion star ascendant, but alas,
The sceptred shade that values earthly might
And power, and pith, and bottom, as the grass,
Gave with his fleshless fist a buffer slight,
Say, bottle-holding Leech, why ends so soon the fight?
What boots to inquire? Tis done, green-mantled Erin
May weep, her hopes of milling sway pass by,
And Cribb, sublime, no lowlier rival fearing;
Repose, sole Ammon of the fistic sky,
Conceited, quaffing his blue ruin high,

Till comes the Swell, that comes to all men must,
By whose foul blows Sir Daniel low doth lie,
Summons the Champion to resign his trust
And mingles his with kings, slaves, chieftains,
   beggar's dust!

'W.W.' ('William Wordsworth') also contributed a poem
to *Blackwood's*, which read, in part:

Yea, even I,
Albeit who never 'ruffian'd' in the ring,
Nor know of 'challenge' save the echoing hills,
Nor 'fibbing' save that poesy doth feign,
Nor hear his fame, but as the mutterings
Of clouds contentious on Helvellyn's side,
Distant, yet deep, aguise a strange regret
And mourn Donnelly – Honourable Sir Daniel
(Blessings be on them, and eternal praise,
The Prince Regent and Dan Donnelly,
The Knighter and the Knighted); love doth dwell
Here is these solitudes, and on corporal clay,
Doth for its season bear the self-same fire,
Impregnate with the same humanities,
Moulded and mixed, like others …

The bogus lamentations of the great poets came from
the fertile imagination of William Maginn, a humorous
Irish poet and journalist who, before becoming editor
of *Fraser's Magazine*, was a regular contributor to *Blackwood's*. The editor of *Blackwood's*, Professor John Wilson

('Christopher North'), published the pieces as a witty and good-natured dig at his friend Pierce Egan's pretence of fine writing. Egan, whose *Boxiana* had been serialized in *Blackwood's*, admitted he was puzzled at the meaning of many of the magazine's tributes to Donnelly. 'We do not understand the gist of them,' he confessed, 'but no doubt they are truly interesting.' He regretted not having the assistance of Bob Gregson, the 'Poet Laureate of the Prize Ring', and he thought that such pugilistic acquaintances as Bill Gibbons and Daniel Mendoza might have been able to decipher the meanings of the Greek and Hebrew poems.

Professor Wilson's own proposed inscription for Donnelly's tombstone was among those rejected:

> Underneath this pillar high
> Lies Sir Dan Donnelly;
> He was a stout and manly man
> And people called him 'Buffing Dan';
> Knighthood he took from George's sword
> And well he wore it, by my word;
> He died at last, for forty-seven
> Tumblers of Punch he drank one even;
> O'erthrown by Punch,
> Unharmed by fist,
> He died undefeated pugilist;
> Such a buffer as Sir Dan
> Ireland will never see again.

Many of the laments published in *Blackwood's* and other periodicals bemoaned the departed champion's love of liquor, such as the following by Morgan O'Doherty:

Majestic Donnelly, proud as thou art,
Like a cedar on top of Mount Hermon,
We lament that Death shamelessly made thee depart
In the gripes, like a blacksmith or chairman.
Oh, hadst thou been felled by Tom Cribb in the ring,
Or by Carter been milled to a jelly,
O, sure that would have been a more dignified thing
Than to kick for a pain in your belly.
A curse on the belly that robbed us of thee
And the bowels unfit for their office;
A curse on the poteen you swallowed so free,
For a stomach complaint, all the doctors agree,
Far worse than a headache or cough is.
Death who, like a cruel and insolent bully, drubs
All those he thinks fit to attack,
Cried 'Dan, my tight lad, try a touch of my
    mulligrubs,'
Which soon laid him flat on his back.

Thomas Jennings, a soda water manufacturer, from Brown Street, Cork, wrote a sorrowful dirge that could be sung to the air of 'Molly Astore':

As down Exchequer Street I strayed a little while ago,
I chanced to meet an honest blade, his face so brimful
    of woe;

I asked him why he seemed so sad, or why he sighed
   so sore;

Oh, Gramachree, och, Tom, says he, Sir Daniel is
   no more.

With that he took me straight away, and pensively
   we went

To where poor Dan's body lay in a wooden waistcoat
   pent,

And many a yard before we reached the threshold of
   his door,

We heard the keeners as they screeched, Sir Daniel is
   no more.

We entered soft, for feelings sad were stirring in our
   breast,

To take farewell of the lad who now had gone to rest;

We took a drop of Dan's poteen and joined the
   piteous roar;

Oh, where shall be his fellow seen, since Daniel is
   no more.

His was the fist whose mighty dint did Oliver defeat,

His was the fist that gave the hint it need not oft repeat,

His was the fist that overthrew his rivals o'er and o'er,

But now we cry, in pillalu, Sir Daniel is no more.

Cribb, Cooper, Carter, need not fear great Donnelly's
   renown,

For at his wake we're seated her while he is lying down,

For Death, the primest swell of all, has laid him on
   the floor

And left us here, alas, to bawl, Sir Daniel is no more.

EPITAPH

Here lies Sir Daniel Donnelly, a pugilist of fame;
In Ireland born and bred was he and he was
    genuinely game;
Then if an Irishman you be, when you have read
    this o'er,
Go home and drink the memory of him, who is
    no more.

The posthumous appraisals of the Irish champion generally found more to appreciate in his character than his fighting ability. Though he remained unbeaten throughout his career, it was felt that he had not fully realized his potential. Obviously a man who had not met his master deserved respect, but most English observers did not share their Irish counterparts' unshakeable belief in his invincibility. The main criticism was that he had failed to take on the cream of English pugilism, such as Cribb, Spring and Carter. It is an argument that is replicated whenever the merits of boxers who never met in the ring are discussed. Comparing the respective records, styles, scientific ability, punching power and resilience of rival boxers proves nothing. Unless they face each other in the ring, no one can say who is the better man. Even then, hot favourites often fall. Upsets are part and parcel of boxing and play a major part in its ongoing fascination. A question often asked is how might the men of the bare-knuckle era have fared if a time machine were to transport them into modern rings? Without a shadow of doubt, they would have been outclassed. Dan Donnelly would not have laid a glove – or a bare fist – on Muhammad Ali. And can anyone imagine him tossing the seven-foot Russian Nicolay Valuev with his favourite cross-buttock?

Pierce Egan noted that Donnelly proved a disappointment to The Fancy in his only fight on English soil, against Tom Oliver. 'He did not look the same as against Cooper,' he observed, 'but was a most dangerous opponent from his great knowledge of throwing.' Stripped for action, Dan Donnelly stood six feet and half an inch and weighed fourteen stone. The English pugilist Jack Scroggins included in his 1827 memoirs a 'table of merit' of leading pugilists. Donnelly was awarded ten out of ten for weight and strength, five for 'bottom' (stamina and courage), two for activity, and just one for skill.

Harold Furniss, editor of *Famous Fights*, declared that Egan was spouting 'high falutin' rubbish' in his assessment of Dan's fighting ability:

> If we are to believe Pierce Egan, 'Sir Daniel' was the greatest fighter that ever lived and, indeed, to this day you will find Irishmen who maintain that England never produced a boxer that was a patch upon the mighty Dan. Well, I am willing to admit that Donnelly was a good man, but, though never beaten, it must be remembered that he was never opposed to such really first-class men as Tom Cribb and Tom Spring, either of whom, in my opinion, would have short work of him.

Percy Sholto Douglas, the 10th Marquis of Queensberry and son of the man who framed the rules of boxing in 1867, gave his assessment of Donnelly's style in an article published in the *Chicago Tribune* in 1912:

> The Irishman had a peculiar style of fighting, holding his head far back and leaning to the right, a pose often seen in the pictures of other old-time fighters. Although an active man and capable of pretty footwork, he seldom retreated. His forte was to stand right up, giving and receiving punishment. He seldom had marks after a fight, and scarcely a scar or disfigurement at the end of his career.

Professor John Wilson concluded that the Irish champion 'seemed happy and contented with the fame he enjoyed under his native skies. It was never his desire to fight on this [English] side of the Channel. He was satisfied with being held as the most formidable buffer, as our good Irish friends denominate pugilists, among the potato-fed population of upwards of five million.'

Dr Shelton Mackenzie, who edited William Maginn's *Luctus on the Death of Sir Daniel Donnelly*, added his own observation:

> We have heard it said that Sir Daniel's style of boxing showed, perhaps too strikingly, that he excelled at the miscellaneous fighting of Donnybrook Fair. He was not a straight or a quick hitter. The death of this illustrious man has left unsolved a problem. Could he have beaten Cribb? Could Carter have beaten him? Alas, vain interrogatories. The glory of Ireland is eclipsed – and ages may pass before another sun shines in what Mr Egan so beautifully calls her pugilistic hemisphere.

There was no doubting Dan's popularity with all sections of the community. The idol of the poor in his native land, he was widely admired by the English aristocracy for his bravery, his personality, his good humour and his clear inclination to live up to the best image of the Irish rogue. T.G. Hazard, in a preface to his book *The Life of Dan Donnelly*, published shortly after the boxer's death, paid a warm tribute to his subject:

> He was brave, yet meek. He was wild, giddy, and heedless of consequences, yet he was noble in his principles, compassionate and quiet. For since he first exhibited his courage, it has not been known that he quarrelled with any person. He would rather bear the most severe injury than retaliate. Yet, if challenged by one who shed the smallest contempt on his country, he displayed the bravery which shall be handed down to posterity.

Pierce Egan probably summed him up better than anyone when he wrote in *Boxiana*:

> Donnelly was a creature of the moment. He was excellent company, creating mirth and laughter all around him. His sayings were droll in the extreme and his behaviour was always decorous. He was generous, good natured and grateful. Tomorrow might, or might not, be provided for and it never created any uneasiness in his mind. He would say 'Devil may care.' He was an Irishman, every inch of him.

Afterword

DONNELLY'S HOLLOW MONUMENT

Some three kilometres from Kilcullen, in County Kildare, as the road enters the Curragh, is Donnelly's Hollow. At its base stands an eight-foot limestone monument marking the scene of Donnelly's famous triumph over George Cooper. Today, only the summer picnickers and grazing sheep occasionally disturb the peace of a spot where, on a cold December day almost 200 years ago, the Irish champion's fans wildly celebrated their hero's victory over his English rival in a battle that lives on in story and in song.

The memorial, unfortunately, has suffered some of the ravages of time, weather and vandals. Nevertheless, it remains a popular stopping-off spot for coach tours and school outings, when the day-trippers take delight in hearing Donnelly's story and literally walking in his footsteps. Had it been left to the Irish, Dan's great victory might never have been commemorated. It was only after a trio of world-famous boxers visited the site in 1887 that the idea of erecting a monument was suggested. The one-and-only John L. Sullivan, reigning heavyweight champion of the world, was on an exhibition tour of Britain and Ireland when he was taken to Donnelly's Hollow.

The great John L. Sullivan, last of the bare-knuckle world heavyweight champions, visited Donnelly's Hollow in 1887 and was among the first subscribers to a fund for Dan's monument.

'The Boston Strong Boy', whose father was from Tralee and his mother from Athlone, was clearly moved by his visit to the historic spot. Another Irish-American, Jake Kilrain, along with Englishman Charley Mitchell, who also had Irish roots, followed Sullivan's trail and it was then that the plan was hatched to formally honour Donnelly's victory. The three prizefighters willingly contributed to a memorial fund and, after the Irish rather shamefacedly matched the generous donations from abroad, enough money was raised for the obelisk to be completed 'in a most artistic and satisfactory manner' by Peter Hynes, of Messrs Farrell and Son, Glasnevin, Dublin.

On the front face of the obelisk, now barely discernible, the following was spelt out in raised letters:

DONNELLY BEAT COOPER ON THIS SPOT, 13TH DEC. 1815

(Below this, on two separate shields:)
Dan Donnelly, born in Dublin 1770. Died 1820.
Geo. Cooper, born in Staffordshire 1791. Died 1834.

(On the left-hand side of the monument:)
Donnelly fought Tom Hall, Tom Oliver.

(On the right-hand side:)
Cooper fought Lancaster, Joy, Molineaux, Robinson, Kendrick.

(On the rear side:)
Erected by public subscription, 1888.

If the date of Donnelly's birth as shown was to be accepted, he was fifty years old when he died. This seems to be well wide of the mark. He was hardly twenty-one years older than Cooper when they fought.

As with the handsome tombstone that once covered his grave in Bully's Acre, the Curragh memorial proved none too popular with British soldiers based at the nearby military camp. It was used as target practice for stones and other missiles. Fortunately, the obelisk proved as indestructible under attack as did Donnelly himself in the ring.

In was not until the 1950s that public interest in Donnelly's Hollow was rekindled, coinciding with the acquisition by Kilcullen publican Jim Byrne Junior of Donnelly's preserved arm, which he put on display in The Hideout tavern. A Donnelly Monument Renovation Committee was formed, under the chairmanship of P. Brady, and an appeal was launched for funds to cover the cost of cleaning up the Hollow and placing a stone tablet at the foot of the memorial. Ignoring the earlier date shown for Dan's birth, the inscription read:

> Dan Donnelly, Champion of Ireland. Born in Dublin, 1788. Occupation: carpenter. Began ring career by beating Tom Hall at the Curragh, Sept. 1814. Hall left the ring in 14th round crying 'Foul'. In December 1815, Donnelly beat George Cooper at the Curragh. Three years later he went to England and challenged all-comers. In a 34-round fight, he beat Tom Oliver with a heavy blow on the ear followed by a cross-buttock.

*The original inscription on the monument in Donnelly's Hollow stated
that the Irish champion was born in 1770. The more generally accepted
date of 1788 was substituted when a stone tablet was installed in 1953.*

The renovation was completed in 1953, the year of
An Tostal, a national festival organized with the support
of the Fianna Fáil government and aimed at lifting public
spirits during a period of severe economic depression.
Throughout the countßry, local committees ran events as
part of the festival and, in Kilcullen, the organizers hit on
a winner when they staged a 'rematch' between Dan Donnelly and George Cooper.

'Dan Donnelly Fights Again' ran the front-page headline in *The Leinster Leader*. The story told of thousands of
excited spectators cramming into Donnelly's Hollow on
the previous Sunday afternoon, 19 April, to witness the
'fight'. If those who paid one to five shillings to stand or

The Irish Press

C   Do Cum Slóipe Dé agup Onópa na héipeann   The Truth in the News.

Vol. XXIII, No. 93.   MONDAY, APRIL 20, 1953.   PRICE 2d.

OLD-TIME FIST BATTLE COMES ALIVE AGAIN IN FAMED DONNELLY'S HOLLOW

Korean Peace Ta Begin Next Sati

First Exc

(REUTER, U

FULL-SCALE Korea
next Saturday, U.N
to-day. At this brief
dropped their demand t
gardless of their wis
previous talks.

The exchange of U
and wounded prisoners

Twelve British, 30 A
cans, four Turks, and one
from the fighting force
Canada, South Africa,
Philippines and Greece w
released in the exchang
be made in two stages.

A Columbia broadcastin
tem broadcast identified t
American disabled captive
returned as Carl Kircher
of New York city. First
prisoner to be exchange
trooper E. O'Donnell w
address at St. Helen's,
shire.

A brisk fight was
about a mile to the west
Communist ambulances rol

Top: *The front page of* The Irish Press *on 20 April 1953 captured the scene in Donnelly's Hollow where Dan's fight with George Cooper 138 years earlier was re-enacted* (bottom).

sit on the historic slopes let their imaginations run free, they might have convinced themselves they were watching the real thing instead of a re-enactment of the famous contest. The crowd quickly got into the spirit of the occasion and cheered almost as heartily as their predecessors back in 1815 as 'Donnelly', played by local amateur boxer Jim Berney, surged into the attack against 'Cooper' (Irish Army Sergeant Kevin McCourt). For further authenticity, members of a Gaelic football club dressed in period costume sat around the ring cheering on 'the Irish champion'. True to history, 'Miss Kelly' (C. Whelan) climbed through the ropes and pleaded with 'Dan' to get up off the ground, as she had bet her entire fortune on him winning. She was 'rescued' from the melee by her brother, 'Captain Kelly' (played by Gerry Kelly).

It was all good clean fun and the spectators took delight in joining in, even if some of them got a bit over-enthusiastic. One of the boxers' seconds was led away from the scene nursing a sore head after getting in the way of a swinging shillelagh. It was only afterwards revealed that the 'fight' almost had to be called off a week earlier when Kevin McCourt suffered damaged ribs in a too-realistic rehearsal. He gallantly agreed to go through with it, much to the relief of the organizers. So successful was the pageant that it was repeated the following year. So, on 16 May 1954, 'Donnelly' and 'Cooper' toed the line once again. The crowd that had come to see a mixture of thrills and farce were not disappointed. Even the notoriously inadequate Broughton Rules of Boxing were ignored and the affair ended up in a good-humoured free-for-all involving boxers, seconds and spectators.

Another re-enactment of the Donnelly v. Cooper fight was staged on 15 August 1982 during a charity 'open day' at Sir Anthony O'Reilly's Castlemartin Estate in County Kildare. Ringsiders dressed in Georgian costumes cheered as 'Donnelly' (Alan Byrne) and 'Cooper' (Francis O'Brien) battled it out, while 'Miss Kelly' (Catherine Carr) tried her best to inspire her hero. Although no actual blood was shed, Sir Anthony, then chairman of the H.J. Heinz Company, was reported to be delighted at the amount of ketchup used.

Once again, the famous fight was the highlight of the South Docks Festival, staged on 27 July 1991 in Lombard Street, Dan's old Dublin neighbourhood. 'Donnelly' (Raymond Keane) and 'Cooper' (Mikel Murfi) arrived by horse-drawn carriage and later the 'winner' was carried shoulder-high to a local pub.

DAN'S PIPE AND JUG SOLD AT AUCTION

Two fascinating mementoes that Donnelly left behind are a large copper jug that he kept at his last pub and a pipe presented to him by his patron, Captain William Kelly, after his victory over Cooper. The items are now in private ownership.

The five-gallon jug has a small plaque attached and bears the inscription 'Sir Dan Donnelly, Irish champion, Pill Lane, 1820'. Its interesting history is recorded in a

A five-gallon spirit jug kept at Donnelly's last Dublin pub bears a plaque with the inscription 'Sir Dan Donnelly, Irish champion, Pill Lane, 1820'.

A silver-mounted pipe presented to Donnelly by his patron, Captain William Kelly, after his victory over George Cooper. Around the rim is inscribed 'Dan'l Donnelly, 13th December 1815' and a small silver plate at the base bears the initials 'D.D'.

letter sent to its purchaser, Henry B. Fottrell, head of a Dublin firm of solicitors, by the auctioneer who conducted its sale:

August 22, 1940

Dear Mr Fottrell,

This old five-gallon copper measure belonged originally to Sir Daniel Donnelly, Irish boxing champion, Dublin. It was used by him in his 'lushing crib' (punch house) in Pill Lane. At the sale of Donnelly's effects in February 1820, it was purchased by Hugh Blaney, 14 Lower Exchange Street and Smock Alley, where it was a showpiece until Blaney's death on August 22nd 1885, aged 95 years. My father, Michael Butler, of 29 Upper Liffey Street and 126, 127, 128 Upper Abbey Street, bought it at Blaney's sale in 1885. Patrick Cooke, auctioneer, Upper Abbey Street, had this sale. Peter Maher, Irish champion, recently deceased, who lived with Dan Murphy in one of my father's cottages in Farrell's Court, off Upper Abbey Street (now the back entrance to Jervis Street Hospital) used try to lift it full with one arm, as Donnelly was reputed to have done frequently.

John Butler,
29 Lower Ormond Quay,
Dublin.

One year later, Donnelly's pipe came up for auction and was also purchased by Henry B. Fottrell. The handsome silver-mounted pipe, almost a foot long, has a silver band around its rim bearing the inscription 'Dan'l Donnelly, 13th Dec 1815' as well as a small silver plate at its base with the initials 'D.D.' Its provenance was traced in a letter from the vendor in response to a request from John Butler:

May 21, 1941

Dear Mr Butler,

All I know of Dan Donnelly's pipe was told me by my mother, who gave it to me with some other oddments. It was after one of Donnelly's fights that souvenir hunters got busy and he distributed odd pieces. His pipe was the last thing left and my father begged so hard he handed it to him for a keepsake. It has been in our possession ever since. I cannot tell you the year but my father is dead now over 60 years.

Miss K. Tierney,

80a Vernon Avenue,

Clontarf,

Dublin.

DONNELLY RECALLED ON STAGE

Pierce Egan, celebrated author of *Boxiana*, also wrote several plays, among them *Life in Dublin, or Tom, Jerry and Logic on their travels*, which opened at the Theatre Royal, Dublin, on 18 February 1834. During act three, four of the characters discuss Irish prizefighters and 'Jerry' sings a song about Dan Donnelly, after which he engages in a sparring session with one of his companions. While the play, more a series of loose episodes relating to places or aspects of Dublin life, hardly stretched the intellect of its audiences, it proved a popular success. It later did the rounds in Britain, including the London Opera House, and was performed as late as 1842. A drama entitled *Dan Donnelly, Champion of Ireland* was enacted on the New York stage in 1870 and included 'a grand realistic re-enactment' of Donnelly's fight with George Cooper. 'Young' Barney Aaron, who played Donnelly, and Sam Collyer, as Cooper, were England-born pugilists who became American lightweight champions.

ENCOUNTER WITH A 'GHOST'

In another of his books, *Every Gentleman's Manual*, published in 1845, Pierce Egan told a creepy story of visiting Donnelly's grave some years after the Irish champion's death. On his arrival at Bully's Acre, he was dismayed to discover that 'the monument has been completely destroyed, bit by bit, and taken away, so that nothing remains of it to be seen but the abutment'. Egan unwisely made the visit around dusk, when the long shadows and the eerie quietness began to play tricks on him. He imagined he saw the grave gaping open and 'the shade of the champion appeared before me, pale and wan'.

'What! My old friend Boxiana,' the apparition addressed him. 'Are you still preserved among the Fancy? No big ones [outstanding prizefighters] these days – rather at fault in that respect. The sporting like to see the big ones in the ring.' As Egan nodded his assent, Donnelly's spectre went on to deplore the introduction of the knife, rather than the fist, to settle even the slightest argument. 'Do all you can, Boxiana, to support the good cause. Continue to encourage pugilism with your pen as a national feature, always advocating a clear stage and fair play, but decry the knife, the dreadful uses of which are found out too late, and the ...' The voice became inaudible and the ghostly figure faded away, leaving Egan to reflect on what he had heard and vowing to back the departed champion's appeal.

A FAVOURITE OF JACK B. YEATS

Renowned Irish artist Jack B. Yeats clearly had an admiration for the Irish champion. He used Donnelly as the subject of three of his pen and ink and watercolours (two reproduced on the covers of this book and the other on page 66). Two of the illustrations were included in *A Broadside*, published by the Cuala Press, Dublin, in August 1910, and the third in *A Broadside*, January 1913. They were later reproduced in *The Different Worlds of Jack B. Yeats: His Cartoons and Illustrations*, by Hilary Pyle, and in *A Little Book of Drawings*, by Yeats. An auction conducted by Whyte's of Dublin on 18 May 2009 saw two of the originals sold for a combined total of €3500. Yeats also produced an oil painting entitled *Donnelly's Hollow* in 1930.

PLAQUE ERECTED AT LAST RESIDENCE

In 1979, Dublin Tourism erected a blue plaque on the front wall of a building to the rear of the Four Courts, marking the site of Donnelly's last pub, where he was landlord at the time of his death in 1820. The address was then 29 Pill Lane, now the junction of Chancery Street and Greek

Street. Comdt. Vincent Horgan, director of Dublin Tourism and a trustee of the Irish Amateur Boxing Association, performed the unveiling, which was attended by former European amateur champions Gearoid O Colmain and Maxie McCullagh along with other members of the Irish Ex-Boxers Association. The plaque was removed in 2009 when the building became vacant.

At the unveiling of a plaque to Dan Donnelly at his last residence in Pill Lane (now Chancery Street) in 1979 were (left to right) *author Patrick Myler, former European amateur boxing champions Gearoid O Colmain and Maxie McCullagh, and Matt McNulty, of Dublin Tourism.*

ELECTED TO HALL OF FAME

In 2008, Dan Donnelly was inducted into the International Boxing Hall of Fame, based at Canastota, New York. He joined the 'Pioneers' section, reserved for those who fought in the bare-knuckle era, before the introduction of gloves. Donnelly is one of seven Irishmen to have gained entry to the Hall of Fame since its inception in 1990. The others are John Morrissey, 'Nonpareil' Jack Dempsey, Jack McAuliffe, Tom Sharkey, Jimmy McLarnin and Barry McGuigan. In 1960, *The Ring* magazine inducted Donnelly into its Boxing Hall of Fame, which no longer exists.

DAN'S ARM ON TOUR

Down the years, Donnelly's preserved right arm has taken on something of a life of its own. The famous American pugilist Jake Kilrain recalled viewing it in a Belfast pub (probably the Duncairn Arms) in 1887. After its transfer to The Hideout in Kilcullen, County Kildare, in 1953, it continued to fascinate visitors for the next fifty years until the pub was sold by Des Byrne, son of the late Jim Byrne Junior. Since Des Byrne's death in 2006, his widow, Josephine, has kept the arm in private ownership. She said: 'I couldn't put a price on it, as the sentimental value is too high. It is something that has been in the family for almost sixty years and is priceless.'

In 2006, James J. Houlihan, a partner in Houlihan-Parnes Realtors of New York and dedicated fight fan, hit on the idea of staging an exhibition honouring the Irish contribution to world boxing history. The Fighting Irish-men exhibition opened at the Irish Arts Center in Manhattan and included such ring memorabilia as John L. Sullivan's fur coat and Jack Dempsey's sports jacket, as well as a heavy bag from Gene Tunney's training camp, plus hundreds of historic photographs, books and posters. Houlihan persuaded Josephine Byrne to let him borrow Donnelly's arm, and Henry Donohue, chief pilot with Aer Lingus, kept the precious relic in the safety of the cockpit on the flight to New York.

Josephine Byrne, current owner of Donnelly's arm, with New York businessman James J. Houlihan, curator of The Fighting Irishmen exhibition, which included the world's most unusual boxing souvenir. Courtesy Brian Byrne.

The exhibition continued to attract streams of visitors when it was switched to another New York venue, the South Street Seaport Museum, and again when it relocated to the John J. Burns Library in Boston College. In 2009, Dan's extended forefinger pointed the way home. The Fighting Irishmen exhibition crossed the Atlantic to the Ulster American Folk Park, just outside Omagh, County Tyrone, where it ran from May to November 2009. The following year, after an absence of almost two centuries, Donnelly – or, more precisely, the remains of his remains – returned to his native city when The Fighting Irishmen exhibition opened at the GAA Museum in Croke Park on 18 May. Once again, visitors were fascinated by the unique display item and wanted to know all about the legendary Irishman and his enduring arm.

'It is one of the oldest and most unique pieces of sports memorabilia,' said Jim Houlihan. 'People who are knowledgeable about boxing have heard about the arm. But to the uninitiated, they think you are kidding until you explain the story.'

Author Patrick Myler, with his children, David, Alan and Gillian,
examining Donnelly's arm in 1976.

Bibliography

BOOKS

Anonymous, *A Monody on the Death of Daniel Donnelly*, Dublin 1820.

Ball, James Moores, *The Sack-'em-Up Men: An Account of the Rise and Fall of the Modern Resurrectionists*, Edinburgh and London 1928.

Batchelor, Denzil, *The Boxing Companion*, London 1964.

Brady, James, *Strange Encounters: Tales of Famous Fights and Famous Fighters*, London 1946.

Bryant, Arthur, *The Age of Elegance 1812–1822*, London 1950.

Buchanan-Taylor, W., assisted by James Butler, *What Do You Know About Boxing?*, London 1947.

Chart, D.A., *The Story of Dublin*, Dublin 1932.

Crean, Rev. Cyril F., editor, *Parish of the Sacred Heart, Donnybrook*, Dublin 1966.

D'Alton, John, *The History of County Dublin*, Dublin 1838.

Edmundson, Joseph, *Great Moments in Boxing*, London 1974.

Egan, Pierce, *Boxiana*, vols 2, 3, 4, London 1818, 1821, 1828.

—, *Every Gentleman's Manual*, London 1845.

Fitzpatrick, William J., *History of the Dublin Catholic Cemeteries*, Dublin 1900.

Fleetwood, Dr John, *The Irish Body Snatchers: A History of Body Snatching in Ireland*, Dublin 1988.

Fleischer, Nat, *The Ring Record Book and Boxing Encyclopaedia*, New York 1962.

Ford, John, *Prizefighting: The Age of Regency Boximania*, Devon 1971.

Grose, Captain Francis, *A Classical Dictionary of the Vulgar Tongue*, third edition, London 1963.

Hazard, T.G., *The Life of Dan Donnelly, Late Champion of Ireland*, Dublin 1820.

Healy, James N., *The Mercier Book of Old Irish Street Ballads, vol. 3, The Irish at Play*, Cork 1969.

Hibbert, Christopher, *George IV, Prince of Wales*, London 1972.

—, *George IV, Regent and King 1811–1830*, London 1973.

Hurley, Jon, *Tom Spring: Bare-Knuckle Champion of All England*, Gloucestershire 2002.

Hyde, Douglas, *Songs and Poems of Raftery*, Dublin 1933.

Igoe, Vivien, *Dublin Burial Grounds and Graveyards*, Dublin 2001.

Joyce, Weston St. John, *The Neighbourhood of Dublin*, Dublin and Waterford 1912.

Little, Dr George A., *Malachi Horan Remembers*, Dublin 1943.

Lynch, Bohun, *The Prize Ring*, London 1925.

MacThomais, Eamonn, *Me Jewel and Darlin' Dublin*, Dublin 1974.

Maxwell, Constanta, *Dublin Under the Georges 1714–1830*, London 1936.

McCall, P.J., *In the Shadow of St Patrick's* (first read as a paper before the Irish National Literary Society on 27 April 1893), Dublin 1894.

McCormick, John B., *The Square Circle, or Stories of the Prize Ring*, New York 1897.

Miles, Henry Downes, *Pugilistica: the History of British Boxing*, vols 1–3, Edinburgh 1880–1906.

O'Broin, Seosamh, *Inchicore, Kilmainham and District*, Dublin 1999.

O Lochlainn, Colm, *Irish Street Ballads*, Dublin 1939.

O'Neill, Capt. Francis, *Irish Minstrels and Musicians*, Chicago 1913.

Prestidge, Dennis, *Tom Cribb at Thistleton Gap*, Leicestershire 1971.

Priestly, J.B., *The Prince of Pleasure and his Regency 1811–1830*, London 1969.

Pyle, Hilary, *The Different Worlds of Jack B. Yeats: His Cartoons and Illustrations*, Dublin 1994.

Reid, J.C., *Bucks and Bruisers: Pierce Egan and Regency England*, London 1971.

Sawyer, Tom, *Noble Art: An Artistic and Literary Celebration of the Old English Prize-Ring*, London 1989.

Shepherd, T.B., compiler, *The Noble Art: An Anthology*, London 1950.

Wignall, Trevor, *Prides of the Fancy*, London 1928.

Yeats, Jack B., *A Little Book of Drawings*, Dublin 1979.

NEWSPAPERS AND PERIODICALS

Blackwood's Magazine, March and May 1820.

Boxing Illustrated, February 1964.

Boxing and Wrestling, January 1965.

Brooklyn Daily Eagle, 2 and 5 May 1870; 27 May 1872.

Carberry's Annual, Christmas 1950.

Carrick's Morning Post, 16, 22 and 24 September 1814; 19 and 23 February 1820.

Chicago Tribune, 11 February 1912.

Dublin Evening Post, 22 February 1820.

Dublin Journal, 18 and 20 September 1819; 1 March 1820.

Dublin Penny Journal, 25 August 1832; 16 November 1833.

Evening Herald, 31 May 1941; 1, 7, 12 and 13 May 1965;
   16 March 1968; 5 September 1970; 29 January 1972.
Famous Fights – Past and Present, II, 14; 3 June 1901; III, 37
   (date unknown).
Freeman's Journal, 19 February and 4 March 1820.
Ireland of the Welcomes, May/June 2009.
Irish Book Lover, XXVIII, February 1942.
Irish Independent, 20 April 1953; 3 March 1961; 17 June 1966.
Irish Journal of Medical Science, February 1929.
Irish Press, 20 April 1953.
Kildare Archaeological Society Journal, III, 1899–1902.
Leinster Leader, 25 April 1953; 16 May 1954.
Mirror of Literature, Amusement and Instruction, 19 September 1829.
National Police Gazette, 2 February 1881.
Nationalist and Leinster Times, 18 and 25 April 1953.
New York Clipper, 5 September 1857.
Saunder's Newsletter, 19 February 1820.
Sporting Magazine, November and December 1815; June 1817;
   March 1820.
Sports Illustrated, 20 February 1995.
Sunday Independent, 19 April 1953.
Sunday Express 'Classic' magazine, 26 March 1995.
Sunday Press, 24 March 1974.
Tuam Herald, 27 September 1930; 24 October 1931.
The Ring, January and September 1961; May 1998.

PROGRAMME
Donnelly's Hollow Pageant, 1954.

MANUSCRIPT
Kelly, Captain William, manuscript number 13,562 in
   National Library of Ireland.

Index

Aaron, 'Young' Barney, 182

Ali, Muhammad, 70, 167

Allardice, Robert Barclay ('Captain Barclay'), 29, 31, 33–4, 36–7, 43, 53, 56, 93–4

Anatomy Act (Second), 8

Austen, Jane, 134

Baer, Max, 43

'Barclay, Captain' *see* Allardice, Robert Barclay

Batts, Johnny, 69–70

Belcher, Tom, 39, 102, 106, 109, 118, 130

Belcher's Hollow (Kildare), 39

'Bellows' (horse), 35

Bergin, Joseph, 7

Bergin, Patrick, 7, 153

Berney, Jim, 177

Black Lion, The (Dublin), 144

Blackwood's Magazine, 6, 119, 160, 162–3

Blaney, Hugh, 180

Blucher, Gebhard Leberecht von, 135

Body snatchers *see* Sack-'em-Ups

Borrow, George Henry, 53

Boru, King Brian, 152

Boxiana, 47, 64, 76, 82–3, 88, 96, 108, 115, 125, 132, 149, 155, 159, 163, 169, 181

Brady, P., 174

Broadside, A, 183

Broughton, Jack, 41

Broughton's Rules (1743), 41, 177

Brummell, Beau, 134

Buchanan-Taylor, W., 117

Bully's Acre (Dublin), 3, 9, 152–3, 155, 174, 182

Burke, James 'Deaf', 32

Burke, William, 9

Burns, Ben, 83, 130

Burrowes, J., 5

Butler, John, 180–1

Butler, Michael, 180

Byrne (publican), 7

Byrne, Alan, 178

Byrne, Charles, 12

Byrne, Des, 185

Byrne, Jim (Junior), 14, 174, 185

Byrne, Josephine, 185–6

Byrne, L., 141

Byrne, Simon, 32

Byron, Lord, 128–9, 134, 146, 160

Capstan Bar, The (Dublin), 77

Carlton House (London), 126

Carney, Joseph P., 14

Carpentier, Georges, 43

Carr, Catherine, 178

Carrick's Morning Post, 5, 6, 46, 150, 159

Carter, Jack, 43, 47, 78–86, 88, 102, 120, 122, 130, 140–2, 144, 158–9, 164–6, 168

Castle Tavern (London), 74, 118, 129

'Chanter' (horse), 35

Chicago Tribune, 168

'Childe Daniel', 160

Childe Harold, 160

Clarence, Duke of *see* William IV

Classical Dictionary of the Vulgar Tongue, A, 58

Coady, Jack, 56

Coburn, Joe, 70–1

'Coburn's Challenge to Heenan', 70

Cody, Patrick, 7

Colles, Dr Abraham, 24

Collyer, Sam, 182

Connery's timber yard (Dublin), 21, 72

Cooke, Patrick, 180

Cooper, George, 5, 14, 34, 51–3, 55–61, 64–9, 71–2, 75–7, 82, 102, 113, 120–1, 138, 140, 142, 154, 158–9, 165, 167, 171, 173–5, 177–8, 182

Cooper, Sir Henry, 131

Cope, Enos, 120

Corbett, James J., 91

Corcoran, Peter, 146

'Cowardly Englishman, The', 71

Crampton, Sir Philip, 10

Crawley Downs (Sussex), 98–9, 101, 112

Cribb, George, 37

Cribb, Tom, 33, 37, 52, 74, 81, 84–5, 87–8, 91, 93–4, 101, 108, 130–1, 158, 161, 164–8

Curwin, J.C., 18

Dalton, John, 153, 155

Dan Donnelly, Champion of Ireland (drama), 182

Dead Watchers, 9

Dempsey, Jack, 43, 186

Dempsey, 'Nonpareil' Jack, 185

Devlin, Anne, 21

Devlin, Arthur, 21–2

Different Worlds of Jack B. Yeats, The, 183

Dispensary for the Sick Poor (Dublin), 24

Dixon, Christopher, 10

Donnelly, Dan: brothers and sisters, 17, 48; father *see* Joseph Donnelly; mother, 17, 48, 62–4, 75; sons, 119, 149; wife, 75, 77, 118–19, 121–2, 147–9; and his Dublin pubs, Capel Street, 78; Coombe, The, 77–8; Pill Lane (Chancery Street), 144, 146, 150–1, 156, 180, 183; Poolbeg Street, 75, 78; knighthood, 125–7, 132, 135–6, 139, 159, 162–3, 165–7, 178, 180

Donnelly, Daniel (grandfather), 19–20

Donnelly, Hugh (uncle), 20

Donnelly, James (uncle), 20

Donnelly, Joseph (father), 17, 20, 25, 62–4

Donnelly, 'Rebecca', 119

Donnelly, Tom (Belfast wine merchant), 14

'Donnelly and Cooper', 67–8

Donnelly's Hollow, 5, 14, 16, 39, 54, 60, 75, 125, 172, 174–5

Donnelly's Hollow (Jack Yeats painting), 183

Donnelly's Hollow monument, 16, 60, 171

'Donnelly's Sprig of Shillelagh', 111–14

Donnybrook Fair, 121–2, 126, 137–8, 141–2, 168

'Donnybrook Fair', 138–9

Donohue, Henry, 186

Dooly, John, 141

Dougherty (pugilist), 39

Douglas, Percy Sholto (10th Marquis of Queensberry), 167

Dowd (pugilist), 111

Dowden, Richard, 157–8

Dowling, W., 141

Doyle, Jack, 43

Dracula, 36

'Drone' (horse), 35

Dublin Directory (1820), 156

Dublin Journal, The, 141

Dublin Penny Journal, The, 61, 137, 152

Duncairn Arms (Belfast), 13, 185

Earl (pugilist), 128

Egan, John 'Bully', 155

Egan, Pierce, 47, 56, 76, 82, 88, 96–7, 101, 108–9, 115, 117, 125, 131, 149, 155, 159, 163, 168–9, 181–3

Emmet, Robert, 21–2, 145

Every Gentleman's Manual, 182

Fallon, John, 78

Famous Fights, 125, 167

Fancy, The, 27, 64, 75, 78, 82, 87, 99–100, 111, 115, 120, 150, 167, 182

Farrell and Son, 173

Fighting Irishmen exhibition, 186–7

Fistiana, 57, 92

Fitzgerald, Lord Edward, 145

Fitzpatrick, P.J., 69

Fives Court, The (London), 87–9

Fleischer, Nat, 16, 127

Ford, William, 102

Fottrell, Henry B., 180

Fraser's Magazine, 162

Freeman, Otway, 34

Freeman's Journal, The, 6, 150

Furniss, Harold, 125, 167

George III, King, 8, 131

George IV, King, 8, 34, 130–1, *see also* Prince Regent

Gerald, Earl of Kildare, 35

Gibbons, Bill, 163

'Glorious Victory of Paddy Murphy, The', 69

Gore family, 20

'Great Victory of John Morrisey over the Russian Sailor Boy, The', 69

Gregson, Bob, 7, 74, 85–6, 120–1, 138, 140, 144, 159, 163

Grose, Captain Francis, 58

Guiccioli, Countess, 129

Gully, John, 33

Hall (surgeon), 12

Hall, Tom, 36–9, 42–7, 55–6, 61, 64, 77–8, 113, 142, 154, 158, 173–4

Halliday, Joseph, 154

Halton, Pat, 143

Hanger, George *see* Lord Coleraine

Hare, William, 9

Harken, Peter, 10

Harmer, Harry, 86, 88, 130

Harvey, Len, 43

Hazard, T.G., 156, 169

Hazlitt, William, 100

'Heenan, the Bold Benicia Boy', 70

Heenan, John C., 70–1

Hicks, Johnny, 35

Hideout, The (Kilcullen), 14, 174, 185

History of County Dublin, The, 153, 155

Hopping, Ned, 102

Horan, Malachi, 31–2

Horgan, Comdt. Vincent, 184

Houlihan, James J., 185–7

Hunter, John, 12

Hynes, Peter, 173

In the Shadow of St Patrick's, 65

International Boxing Hall of Fame (Canastota, New York), 185

Irish Minstrels and Musicians, 35

Irving, Sir Henry, 36

Jackson, 'Gentleman' John, 74, 128

Jennings, Thomas, 164

Johnson, Tom, 74

Joy (pugilist), 173

Keane, Raymond, 178

Kelly, Colonel Edward, 35

Kelly, Gerry, 177

Kelly, Miss, 32, 65, 68

Kelly, Peter, 7

Kelly, Colonel Ponsonby, 35

Kelly, Captain Waldron, 35

Kelly, Captain William, 29, 31–7, 43–4, 53, 65, 178

Kendrick, Black, 102, 173

Kilrain, Jake, 173, 185

King, Tom, 70

Kirby, John, 9

Lamb, Lady Caroline, 134

Lancaster, Harry, 102, 173

Langan, Jack, 91, 94–5, 143

Lashbrook (pugilist), 111

Lavengro, 53

Leinster Leader, The, 175

'Liberty Boys, The', 17

Life in Dublin, 181

Life in London, 101

Life of Dan Donnelly, The, 156, 169

Little, Dr George A., 31

Little Book of Drawings, A, 183

London Prize Ring Rules (1853), 42

Lord Chamberlain, 130

Lord Coleraine (George Hanger), 125

Lord Lieutenant of Ireland (1st Earl Talbot of Hensol), 127

Luctus on the Death of Sir Daniel Donnelly, 168

McAlevey, Hugh 'Texas', 13–14

McAuliffe, Jack, 185

McCall, P.J. (author), 65

McCall, P.J. (stud owner), 33–4

McCourt, Kevin, 177

McCullagh, Maxie, 184

McDonald, Arthur, 20

McGuigan, Barry, 185

Mackenzie, Dr Shelton, 168

McLarnin, Jimmy, 185

Mace, Jem, 71

Maginn, William, 162, 168

Maher, Peter, 180

Malachi Horan Remembers, 31

Marquis of Queensberry Rules (1867), 42

Martin, Sam, 88

Mendoza, Daniel, 39, 163

Miles, Henry Downes, 16

Minor Theatre (London), 83, 88–9

Mirror of Literature, The, 126

Mitchell, Charley, 173

Modern Art of Boxing, The, 39

Molineaux, Tom, 51, 82, 84, 173

Monody on the Death of Dan Donnelly, A, 158

Moran, Michael ('Zozimus'), 10

Morissey, John, 71–2, 185

Murfi, Mikel, 178

Murphy, Dan, 180

Murphy, Paddy, 69

Murrough, Prince, 152–3

Napoleon, 50

Neat, Bill, 102, 120

Ney, Michel, 135

'North, Christopher' *see* Wilson, Prof. John

O'Brien, Francis, 178

O Colmain, Gearoid, 184

O'Connell, Daniel, 14, 145

O'Doherty, Morgan, 6, 164

O'Donnell (pugilist), 62

Oliver, Tom, 21, 82, 88, 91–2, 97, 99, 102–11, 113, 116, 120, 128, 130, 154, 158, 165, 167, 173

O'Neill, Captain Francis, 35

O'Reilly, Sir Anthony, 178

Orford, Catherine, 36

Ormond Boys, the, 17

Painter, Ned, 43, 56, 77, 91, 102, 120

Peacock Theatre (London), 83

Pitt, William (the Younger), 33

Prendergast, P.J., 34

Priestly, J.B., 134

Prince of Pleasure and his Regency, The, 134

Prince of Wales, 69, *see also* Prince Regent

Prince Regent (George IV), 5, 123, 125–30, 132–4, 162

Pugilistica, 16

Pyle, Hilary, 183

Raftery, Antoine, 62

'Rakes of Kildare, The', 61

Randall, Jack, 74, 88, 102

Red Lion, The (London), 91, 111, 120

Regan (innkeeper), 79–80

resurrectionists, 6, 8, *see also* Sack-'em-Ups

Richard II, King, 131

Richmond, Bill, 53, 74, 86, 120, 130

Ring, The, 185

Ring Record Book, The, 16, 127

Robinson (pugilist), 173

Romany Rye, The, 53

Royal Cockpit (London), 101

Royal College of Surgeons (Dublin), 10, 24

Royal College of Surgeons (London), 12

Sack-'em-Ups, 3, 9–10, *see also* resurrectionists

Saunder's Newsletter, 150

Sayers, Tom, 70

Scott, Sir Walter, 141

Scroggins, Jack, 167

Sellars, Harry, 146

Sharkey, Tom, 185

Shelton, Tom, 101, 106, 109

Shepherd (pugilist), 72

Shining Daisy, The (Dublin), 144

Sick and Indigent Roomkeepers' Society (Dublin), 24

'Sir Dan Dann'ly, the Irish Haroe', 126

Small, Bernie, 13

Sporting Magazine, The, 64, 76, 152

Spring, Tom, 74, 84–5, 89–90, 102, 120, 129–31, 166–7

Stoker, Bram, 36

'Stony Pockets', 10

'Sugar Cane Man, The', 65–6

Sullivan, John L., 172–3, 186

Sutton, Harry, 85–7, 120

Thompson (pugilist), 72

Tierney, Miss K., 181

Toastal, An, 14, 175

Topp (painter), 158

Townsend Street (Dublin), 17, 20, 22, 26, 48, 61, 75, 78, 137, 152

Traynor (publican), 7

Tunney, Gene, 186

Tyne, Tom, 128

Union Arms, The (London), 74

Valuev, Nicolay, 167

Ward, Joe, 74

Weekly Dispatch, The (London), 120

Wellington, Duke of, 50, 134–5

Westmoreland (or Lock) Hospital (Dublin), 20

What Do You Know About Boxing?, 117

Whelan, C., 177

White Horse, The (London), 118

Whitelaw, Revd James, 19

Whyte's (auctioneers), 183

Wilberforce, William, 134

William IV, King (Duke of
    Clarence), 101, 129

Wilson, Prof. John ('Christopher
    North'), 119, 163, 168

Winter, Thomas *see* Tom Spring

Wolfe Tone, Theobold, 145

Wordsworth, William, 134, 162

'Yankee Clipper, The', 72

Yeats, Jack B., 183

'Zozimus' (Michael Moran), 10